The Villas of Palladio

Donata Battilotti

The Villas of Palladio

Electa

Translation
Richard Sadleir

Photographic Credits
Amministrazione Provinciale,
Vicenza
Archivio Electa, Milan
Azienda Promozione Turistica,
Rovigo
Centro Internazionale di Studi
di Architettura Andrea Palladio,
Vicenza
Scala, Florence

On cover
Villa Almerico Capra, called La Rotonda (Vicenza).

New edition 1995

Contents

Andrea Palladio

This great architect, whom we associate above all with Vicenza, was actually born in Padua, in 1508. We then hear of him in Vicenza, where his father had placed him in a workshop as an apprentice stonecarver, from which he twice ran away, for reasons unknown to us. And it was in Vicenza that the stonemason Andrea, the son of Pietro della Gondola, was to become the renowned Andrea Palladio. He worked for years in the city as a nameless underlining for the master builders Girolamo Pittoni and Giovanni da Porlezza, the owners of the most prominent building firm in the city at that time.

However, his natural talents and the decisive meeting with Giangiorgio Trissino enabled him to become the firm's architectural expert by the mid-1530s. Trissino was a classicist who supported rigorous adherence to the classical genres in literature and was one of the most active figures in the language controversy of the early Cinquecento. He came of a noble family of Vicenza, anti-Venetian by tradition, and had lived in the most illustrious courts of Italy. He is a key figure in the Vicentine nobility's new awareness that they possessed a cultural identity of their own, in opposition to that of Venice, unloved but dominant. This awareness appeared symbolically in the desire to renew their city, not by imitating Venetian architecture as hitherto, but on the model of Roman classicism.

Andrea and Trissino probably met when the latter, an amateur architect, was restructuring his suburban villa at Cricoli, to a design which appears to have reproduced Raphael's plan for the Villa Madama in Rome, obtained through Sebastiano Serlio; in the humble stonecarver he recognized the future agent of the renewal he so deeply desired. Trissino introduced him to the study of Vitruvius and classical architecture and helped him in his progress; he accompanied him early in 1541 on his first important journey to Rome—others followed in 1545, 1546-1547, in 1549 and 1554—where he was finally able to see and make a survey of the remains of ancient monuments. And finally it was Trissino that gave Andrea his new name, Palladio—the angelic messenger in his interminable epic, *L'Italia liberata dai Goti*—and probably introduced him into the humanist circle of Alvise Cornaro during his sojourn in Padua. Cornaro was the patron of Ruzzante and the inspiration behind the Veronese architect Gian Maria Falconetto's invention of the splendid loggia and odeum for his house at Santo in Padua and his Villa dei Vescovi at Luvigliano, among the earliest Renaissance works in the Veneto. Cornaro provided a valuable counterweight to Trissino's dogmatism and arid theorizing. He believed architecture should be based on a harmonious interplay between decorum and convenience and insisted on the value of practical experiment: these qualities combined with Palladio's long apprenticeship to the craft of building, strengthening and broadening it. All through his career as an architect, Palladio kept a firm hold on the practical problems of building and work on the site, so freeing his works from an over-rigid classicism.

Palladio rejected none of the influences offered by the circles he moved in: his reading of Vitruvius and the great Quattrocento theorist Giambattista Alberti, the traditional architecture of the Veneto and ancient Roman architecture, which he had seen not only in Rome but also Vicenza (which possesses the remains of a Roman theatre at Berga), Verona, Pola, and many other places. He also studied the work of his great contemporaries: Raphael, Donato Bramante, Baldassare Peruzzi, the Sangallos, Sebastiano Serlio, Giulio Romano, Michele Sanmicheli, Jacopo Sansovino, Michelangelo, and later Pirro Ligorio and Vignola. But his architecture is a distillation of all these influences and his works give one the impression of being wholly independent and original.

In the later 1530s Palladio began to receive commissions from the aristocracy of Vicenza and—though he still worked for the "bottega di Pedemuro," its name taken from the neighbourhood where it stood—he designed the villa of the Godi family at Lonedo and the town house of the Civena (1540) at Ponte Furo. At first his commissions were mainly for country houses, perhaps on the model of Trissino at Cricoli. Before the desired transformation could renew the city a dress rehearsal was called for, and the chance came in 1543, with the entrance of the Bishop Niccolò Ridolfi to the city: the streets and squares along the ceremonial route were transfigured by classical structures made out of wood and *pa-*

pier-mâché. Soon after, work began on real buildings. The first public commission that came Palladio's way was for reconstructing the exterior of the Gothic Palazzo della Ragione (1546-1549), known as the Basilica, after the structure built by Formenton (1481-1494) had collapsed and the ideas and designs of other eminent architects—Michele Sanmicheli, Giulio Romano, Jacopo Sansovino and Sebastiano Serlio—had been shelved. The double loggia of white marble, repeating the motif of the *serliana*, runs right round the building. (Construction work continued into the next century.) The result was a design of great evocative power which also imparted an impulse to renew the layout of the squares surrounding it. Twenty-five years later (circa 1565 and 1571) Palladio was commissioned to erect a building opposite it, this time the loggia, with its gigantic order, of the Palazzo del Capitanio (the "Capitanio" was, like the Podestà, a representative of the Venetian government), with exuberant sculptural decorations that celebrate the Christian victory over the Turks at Lepanto.
At the same time new private palaces were also being built: Palazzo da Monte in the Santa Corona *contrada* (1541-1545); Palazzo Thiene at Santo Stefano (1546); Palazzo Iseppo-Porto in Vicenza (1549); Palazzo Chiericati at Isola (1550); the façade of the home of the *notaio* Pietro Cogollo on the Corso (1559-1562); and that of Bernardo Schio in *borgo* Pusterla (1560-1561). And later on the Palazzo Valmarana in Corso Fogazzaro (1565), Palazzo Barberano in *contrà* Porti (1569-1570), and the Palazzo Porto and Palazzo Thiene in Piazza Castello, which were completed by Pietro Scamozzi. And these are only the most important of the many that were built and still exist. Palladio never "gutted" the mediaeval urban fabric with large-scale operations, but his work, though quantitatively limited, proved qualitatively subversive, because it created immensely potent focal points that determined the city's subsequent development.
It should also be said that the immense cost of these projects condemned many of them to go no further than the design stage, and Palladio himself lived to see very few built to completion. By the later 1570s the initial impulse was failing and there followed a period of stasis, almost of defeat. And it was at this moment that the Accademia Olimpica—a circle of noblemen and artists founded in 1555, of which Palladio was a member—decided to build a theatre on its premises. Drawing on his archaeological studies and earlier work with temporary structures, Palladio, on the eve of his death, designed a theatre completely foreign to the contemporary tradition by going back to the ancient Roman theatres (though its uniqueness was partly disguised by Vincenzo Scamozzi, who was responsible for its completion). And the proscenium of the Teatro Olimpico, with niches for the statues of the academicians themselves and an architectural stage-set depicting a mythical Thebes (for the performance of *Oedipus Rex* by Sophocles at the inaugural performance in 1585) embodies a dream of Vicenza in the eyes of the local nobility, their image of themsalves and their long-desired urban renewal.
Palladio was also active outside the Vicenza area. The fame of his victory in the competition for the loggias of the Basilica and the contacts he made with the help of Trissino and, probably, Cornaro inevitably gave him the entrée to Venice and the other cities of the Republic.
From the start, Palladio's relations with Venice were not easy. It appears that a kind of Palladian party was formed, which tried from the 1550s on to obtain official commissions for him, and when they eventually succeeded it was only conditionally and after the death in 1570 of Jacopo Sansovino, the "proto" or superintendent of building in the San Marco area. Palladio's supporters were a group of noblemen led by Marcantonio and Daniele Barbaro, the Contarini, Cornaro, Foscari and Mocenigo families, and others who were working towards a renewal of the oligarchical republican institutions and had close ties with Roman circles. They must have felt the Palladian style to be sufficiently imperial to express the authoritarian ideals they were pursuing. For the same reasons Palladio's uncompromising style—never changed to look more "Venetian" or to suit his patrons—aroused misgivings in many people, especially the conservative class in power, because it seemed to undermine the value and the distinctive features of the Venetian *forma urbis*, which they considered, together with the

B. Picart, Portrait of Andrea Palladio, engraving after a painting attributed to Paolo Veronese (in G. Leoni, The Architecture of A. Palladio in Four Books, London, 1721).
Title page of the "Quattro Libri dell'Architettura" by Andrea Palladio, Venice, 1570.

city's unique political institutions, the symbol of its greatness.

The result was that they commissioned Palladio to build splendid villas on the mainland but not a single palace in the city, let alone projects in the political and economic heart of the Republic, like the new Rialto bridge (1554), the city's true forum on the Grand Canal, or the extensive rebuilding of the elevation of the Doge's Palace facing San Giorgio, following the fire of 1577. Palladio's work in Venice was limited to ephemeral structures, like a wooden theatre for the Compagnia della Calza (1564-1565) or the design of the decorations to celebrate Henry III of Valois's entry to the Lido in 1574, or work located within religious buildings, like the Convent of Santa Maria della Carità (1561) on the outskirts of the city. The latter group included a series of churches in which Palladio achieved a sophisticated interplay of the different orders in the elevations and façades. They range from the elevations of San Pietro al Castello (1558, never built) and San Francesco della Vigna (1562) to the three churches ranged opposite St. Mark's square, on the Giudecca, whose cupolas and slender towers form a stunning visual backdrop: the churches of San Giorgio (1565) the Redentore (1576-1577) and the Zitelle (1579-1580).

On the mainland (and excluding the villas in the countryside) Palladio left works in Verona (Palazzo della Torre, 1561, half destroyed), Udine (Palazzo Antonini and the Bollani arch of 1556), Feltre (the ground-floor loggia of the town hall, 1557), Cividale (town hall, 1564-1565), San Daniele di Friuli (Porta Gemona, 1579). Obviously there were also countless requests for consultancy work within and without the Venetian Republic, such as the Palazzo della Loggia and cathedral of Brescia and the cathedrals of Bergamo, Milan and San Petronio of Bologna, to cite only the most important.

Lastly it should be remembered that Palladio was recognized as a master of hydraulic engineering—he is known to have invented a machine for raising water from great depths—which brought commissions for numerous bridges. One of the most memorable is the bridge of Bassano (1569), destroyed on a number of occasions but always rebuilt to the original design.

In his long and fertile career Palladio did not confine himself to designing buildings; he was also very active as a theorist, culminating in the publication of the *Quattro Libri dell'Architettura* (1570), which followed two descriptive works published in 1554 on *L'antichità di Roma* and the *Descritione de le chiese di Roma*, and preceded an introduction to an Italian translation of Caesar's *Commentaries* (1574-1575). In addition he wrote a study of the *castramentatio* of Polybius which was left unfinished and other manuscript fragments. The *Quattro Libri*, considered the epitome of Palladio's ideas, was immensely influential both in Italy and abroad. They were the fruit of two decades of work, frequently abandoned and resumed, which was begun in about 1550 when Palladio was working on the interpretation of the texts and the illustrations of the *Dieci Libri di Architettura di M. Vitruvio*, published in 1556 by Daniele Barbaro. Palladio's work follows the customary Cinquecento scheme for a treatise, with sections on the architectural orders, the techniques and materials of construction, the different types of building, and the study of ancient Roman monuments, while the second book contains most of his own designs for buildings down to 1570. It has been shown that these are not the actual designs presented to the clients but subsequent refashionings of them to fit the didactic purpose of his book, hence a presentation of different architectural types which had grown out of his personal experience but were open to further variation. Since the illustrations emphasize Palladio's programmatic classical phase, the treatise might give the reader a distorted and partial impression of his work unless it is closely compared with the buildings he actually constructed.

His later years were embittered by the deaths in 1572, at a short interval from each other, of two of his beloved children, Leonida and Orazio (the others were named Silla, Marcantonio and Zanobia, born of his marriage to Allegradonna of Vicenza in about 1534). He died on August 19, 1580, the place of his death being unknown—perhaps in Venice, or Maser or Vicenza. So died the great architect, modestly and discreetly, as he had lived. Most of his fellow Academicians were unable to return from their country houses in time, and he was hurriedly buried on August 25 in Vicenza, in the church of Santa Corona.

Essential Bibliography

Books on Palladio are legion; here I shall cite the most important monographs and some recent studies. For a fuller treatment see Puppi, 1973, brought down to 1982 in the German edition (Puppi, 1982). Also an important contribution to the subject are the bulletins of the Centro Internazionale di Architettura "Andrea Palladio," in Vicenza (bulletin of the C.I.S.A.) and, for individual works, the volumes of the *Corpus Palladianum*. Magrini, 1845; Dalla Pozza, 1943; Zorzi, 1959; Pane, 1961; Wittkower, 1964; Forssman, 1965; Zorzi, 1965; Ackerman, 1966; Ivanoff, 1967; Zorzi, 1967 and 1969; Timofiewitsch, 1968; Rosci, 1970; AA.VV., 1973; Puppi, 1973; Barbieri, 1974; Fancelli, 1974; Burns, 1975; Battilotti, 1977; Berger, 1978; Puppi, 1978 and 1979; Kubelik, 1979; Battilotti, 1979-1980 and 1980; AA.VV., (I, II, III, IV, V, VI), 1980; Cevese, 1980; Magagnato-Marini, in Palladio, 1980; Rigon, 1980; Lewis, 1981; Olivieri, 1981; AA.VV., 1982; Puppi, 1982; Foscari-Tafuri, 1983; Barbieri G., in Palladio, 1988; Zaupa, 1989.

The Palladian Villas

The Palladian Villas or more generally the villas of the Veneto region are not merely works of architecture but closely related to the historical, economic and political life of the area. So we need to take a step back in time to understand the early development of this "country house culture" which transformed the Veneto and made it famous all over the world.

In 1509 the noble Venetian Girolamo Priuli noted in his diary that his fellow-citizens were beginning to abandon sea voyages and overseas trade and "inebriated [were buying] houses and land in the countryside, paying double their true value for them... and on these properties they were building palaces or villas which were extremely costly... and there was no citizen or nobleman that had not bought at least one such estate and house on the mainland... for his recreation."

These words, tinged with a certain bitterness, record a change taking place in Venetian society. More than a century had passed since, in 1404-1405, the Venetian Republic, which had previously controlled only a narrow strip of the Adriatic mainland, eliminated all the various *signorie* lying further inland with a series of military and political actions, and so extended its control over a vast area bounded roughly by the Po to the south and the Oltremincio to the west.

After decades of warfare, a new era began for the Veneto; a period of peace unparalleled in the rest of Italy, during which even the countryside was secure. The feudal-style local nobility was forced to repress its warlike impulses on pain of the loss of all their property, so they began to devote their energies to administering their estates, the principle source of their wealth. At the same time the Venetian aristocracy began to invest in real estate in the subject territories, though their properties were not profitable and served only as a way of employing the wealth obtained from overseas trade. Venice still looked eastwards, until a series of far-reaching events in the latter half of the century began to undermine its dominion of the sea. First Constantinople fell to the Turkish advance (1452), followed by Trebizond (1461) and the island of Negroponte (1470). These losses were a severe blow to Venetian trade, and the situation was aggravated shortly after with the discovery of America and the diminished importance of the Mediterranean, leading to the inevitable decline of the Venetian Republic. New fields in which to assert its power had to be sought and as early as 1454 the Peace of Lodi ratified its desire to become one of the leading mainland Italian states. Soon after (1460) the Council of Ten decreed that detailed maps should be made of its territories, establishing their main features and especially the waterways, the principle lines of communication. But it was not until the dark years of the War of the League of Cambrai that there was a decisive change in Venice's attitude to her mainland territories. To halt her expansion, numerous Italian and foreign states formed an alliance led by Pope Julius II (1508) and Venice found herself isolated, with the enemy armies at the mouth of the lagoon. The territories she lost were all regained by 1517 by skilful diplomatic manoeuvres, and thereafter she regarded the territories as an integral part of the state and essential to her survival. Alliances were formed with the local nobility (most of whom had gone over to the enemy during the war), the bureacracy was reorganized and key points were fortified more effectively. This was accompanied by a transition from traditional forms of commerce to farming on the lands which the nobility had acquired in the previous century.

This was a kind of "silent revolution" which transformed the Venetian territories in the mid-sixteenth century. The state backed up private enterprise in large-scale reclamation of marshy and unproductive estates and introduced more efficient methods of cultivation. These policies were ratified in 1556 by the creation of the Magistracy for Untilled Lands, whose most energetic supporter was Alvise Cornaro himself, who presented the ownership of land and the arts of "sacred agriculture" as ways to give new life to Venice.

The outstanding result of these developments was a kind of "re-feudalization" of the area, epitomized in the proliferation of country houses, the essential infrastructure to enable the landowners to administer their estates. This is not to say that villas did not exist earlier in the Veneto, of course, but they were used mainly as holiday homes where city-dwellers could spend their leisure time.

Villa Godi (Lonedo di Lugo Vicentino), view of the loggia with frescoes by Gualtiero Padovano.

This kind of villa had illustrious precedents, like Petrarch's home at Arquà and, more recently, Caterina Cornaro's country house Barco, at Altivole. And the tradition continued—for example with the Palladian villas known as La Rotonda and La Malcontenta; but in addition to recreation there were new functional needs calling for a different kind of building. And it was these different kinds of requirements that Palladio understood and satisfied. His ideas were naturally not born out of nothing. Their roots lay in earlier developments and they were guided by the teachings of Giangiorgio Trissino and above all Alvise Cornaro. But the final result was wholly due to his own genius.

The villas built in the Quattrocento, especially in the Vicenza area, where the aristocracy retained more markedly feudal qualities, were not built to a single standard type but differed depending on the model they followed, which might be old castles, abbeys, early suburban houses—like those built on the islands of the lagoon, Murano or the Giudecca, for example. In a few decades they even transferred the model of an urban building—perhaps the Venetian *casa-fondaco*, a combination of warehouse and dwelling—to their mainland estates. But there was a feature common to the layout of all these different forms and it is present right from the start, serving a practical purpose: this was the central atrium with a portico or loggia on the façade to bring light and air into the building and allow the countryside to be *possessed* visually. Having recovered from the crisis caused by the League of Cambrai, in the years around 1535 the Quattrocento villa began to be renewed in the Roman classical style, though without introducing new lay-

Villa Caldogno (at Caldogno), room with frescoes by Giambattista Zelotti and workshop (in the large panel: an episode from the Stories of Sofonisba) and Gianantonio Fasolo.

Villa Caldogno (at Caldogno), chamber with frescoes by Gianantonio Fasolo (below the arches: Invitation to the Dance and Game of Cards).

Villa Poiana (Pojana Maggiore), front elevation. *Villa Emo (Fanzolo di Vedelago), front elevation.*

Villa Barbaro (Maser), front elevation.

outs. This was the case with Giangiorgio Trissino's villa at Cricoli near Vicenza, where the man of letters improvised as an amateur architect: actually he did no more than remodel the Quattrocento façade (between about 1535 and 1537) which had been hemmed in between two towers with a gallery below. The house had been built by a Venetian family called Badoer on the model of the *casa-fondaco*. Its façade was rebuilt to a design of Roman and classical inspiration passed to Trissino by Sebastiano Serlio, who later published it as purportedly the original plan for the Villa Madama in Rome.

A far more modern and lucid design—though still only in externals—appeared in the years around 1540. It was the work of Michele Sanmicheli, who designed a villa for the humanist Agostino Brenzoni at Punta San Vigilio (now the Villa Guarienti) on Lake Garda and another villa, now unluckily destroyed, for the Soranzo family at Treville, near Castelfranco, known to us only through surveys from the sixteenth and seventeenth centuries. But a real advance came with the conception of a new kind of building intended for an aristocratic family which had moved from the city to oversee its country estate. The architect was Jacopo Sansovino and the villa was built in about 1538-1540 for the Garzoni, a Venetian family, at Pontecasale in the Paduan countryside. Sansovino was Florentine by birth but Venetian by adoption, and he repeated the stock Quattrocento forms, with a central loggia and flanking blocks but transformed it totally through a classical vocabulary to embody the owners' sense of their own importance and tastes. But the outstanding feature was the creation of a service complex, classical in style and imposing in scale, clearly marked off from the main structure by a wall. Palladio took up Sansovino's ideas and modified them. He experimented with a variety of layouts, as appears from his earliest work: the villa built for the Godi family at Lonedo in about 1537, which opens the series, was followed by villas for the Valmarana family at Vigardolo and for the Gazzotti at Bertesina, the Villa Forni at Montecchio Precalcino and Villa Pisani at Bagnolo, down to the Villa Saraceno at Finale and Villa Caldogno at Caldogno. The experimentation is also evident in a series of early drawings. The starting point was still the local style of country house, and in fact most of the commissions he received were to modernize Quattrocento buildings of this very kind. He retained the portico in the front elevation between two solid blocks, which sometimes were actually derived from castle turrets (as at Bagnolo), and he was very sparing of classical elements, even after his first trip to Rome in 1541. But even Villa Godi has an interesting layout, articulated functionally around a central atrium and hall, linking the front and rear of the building and relating it to the surrounding countryside. These early experiments also develop the motif of the pediment set over the central element in the elevations, which was to become a constant feature of subsequent designs, Palladio derived it from the classical temple and applied it to secular architecture as a way of symbolizing and exalting the aristocratic dignity of the owner. In this early phase, rustic structures and outhouses were not usually handled in this way; yet even as early as the design for Bartolomeo Pagliarino—prior to 1545—as well as at the Villa Thiene at Quinto (1546) and Villa Poiana at Pojana Maggiore (1549-1550), they were carefully designed. Even though they were still separated by a wall from the courtyard of the "manor house," they were skilfully laid out and enhanced by classical porticoes. A decisive innovation appeared at the Villa Angarano (at Angarano), designed in 1548 after Palladio's protracted stay in Rome during 1546-1547.

The main block seems never to have been built—all we have is the illustration in the *Quattro Libri*—unlike the outhouses which were conceived as enclosing the manor court without any break in the unity of the whole, so fusing the functional structures needed for the farm with the main block and providing for the aristocratic owner's leisure while expressing his public image. The high point of this kind of villa-farm, the true mirror of the ideals of the age, appears both in the scale and quality of the design of the Villa Badoera at Fratta Polesine and the Villa Emo at Fanzolo (to mention only edifices fully completed), which are almost small townships. The core of the complex is naturally the temple-residence of the estate-owner, enhanced by its imposing staircase and hallmark pediment, borne on the columns of the loggia and

Villa Barbaro (Maser), the nymphaeum.

richly frescoed on its inner side. On either side of the central composition, subordinated to it but still an important presence, stretch away the colonnades containing barns and outhouses, like arms reaching out into the countryside—sometimes straight, in other cases set at right angles or in a semicircle—often topped with turrets serving as dovecotes. In their shelter the landowner could oversee the work of the labourers, whose homes are scattered over the estate, and keep an eye on the crops, stables, cowsheds and farm equipment.

The various elements of this "township" were fused in a common classical vocabulary and arranged in a precise hierarchy. There is only one case of their being placed all on a single plane, without any distinction between the villa and the functional structures, in the Villa Repeta at Campiglia dei Berici (c. 1557-1558), which has unfortunately not survived. The unusual arrangement here reflected the convictions of Palladio's client, a member of the Anabaptist circles in Vicenza.

The villa-farm model includes the Villa Barbaro at Maser (c. 1554), though here the client's humanist and literary notions of leisure dominate the design, with a flower garden and the magniloquent transfiguration of the outhouses. But alongside this type, in 1553 Palladio designed the twin villas of the Pisani family at Montagna and the Cornaro family at Piombino Dese, so creating a new kind of suburban edifice. It retained the urban palace's layout on two *piani nobili*, but at the same time also had two open galleries facing out into the countryside. This design met the need to create an image of the owner's tastes and also provide a retreat for his leisure-time. They are set in towns and there are no outhouses, or at least these are not part of the composition. This is also the case at the Villa Foscari at Malcontenta, not far from Venice, with the giant order of its imposing pronaos reflected in the waters of the Brenta canal. (A concept foreshadowed at Villa Chiericati at Vancimuglio, 1554.) In the celebrated Rotonda, near Vicenza, functional needs also take

Villa Barbaro (Maser), central chamber, the short "arm," with frescoes by Paolo Veronese.

second place to the desire to celebrate the owner's ideals. This is carried to an extreme here, being embodied in the centralized layout focused on the circular living-room with its crowning cupola. Though this is one of Palladio's most interesting works, it deviates markedly from the ideals that informed his most authentic villas. In fact, after three decades of devotion to this concept, Palladio seems to have encountered difficulties in handling this theme in the later 1560s; this could well be because his own cultural outlook no longer corresponded to the desire for blatantly triumphal and celebratory tones now widespread among potential clients, which would have destroyed the subtle balance that reconciled the city gentleman with the country gentleman, achieved in so masterly a fashion in the Villa Badoer and Villa Emo. The complex partially completed for Marcantonio Sarego at Santa Sofia di Pedemonte (ca. 1565) already betrays a certain over-emphasis that upsets the original layout to create an idealized image of a Roman house. The Villa Porto at Molina di Malo (1572), barely begun and then abandoned, seems to have been based on the same idea, after which, as far as is known, Palladio never designed another villa.

Essential Bibliography

Burger, 1909; Masson, 1955; Franco, 1956; Langenskiöld, 1960; Ackerman, 1963; Mazzotti, 1963; Rupprecht, 1964; Ackerman, 1966, pp. 17-37; Muraro, 1966; Rosci, 1966; Rupprecht, 1966; Ackerman, 1967; Bieganski, 1968; Rosci, 1968; Rupprecht, 1968; Bieganski, 1969; Cevese, 1969; Forssman, 1969; Heydenreich, 1969; Puppi, 1969; Rigon, 1969; Rosci, 1969; Tafuri, 1969; Ventura, 1969; Wolters, 1969; Zancan, 1969; Zorzi, 1969; Barbieri, 1970; Bentmann-Müller, 1970; Cevese, 1971; Puppi, 1971; Bentmann- Müller, 1972; Bieganski, 1972; Barbieri, 1973; Forssman, 1973; Prinz, 1973; Puppi, 1973, in part. pp. 31-35; Suitner Nicolini, 1973; Burns, 1975; Magnani Cianetti, 1976; Kubelik, 1977; Corboz, 1978; Muraro, 1978; Coffin, 1979; Bieganski, 1980; Puppi, 1980; Rigon, 1980, pp. 11-15, 38-42; Soragni, 1980; Muraro, 1981-1982; Canova, 1985; Muraro, 1986; Bödefeld-Hinz, 1987.

Villa Foscari (Gambarare di Mira), view from the canal.

Villa Foscari (Gambarare di Mira), rear elevation.

Following pages:

Villa Almerico Capra, La Rotonda (Vicenza), view of the villa in its setting.

22

The following study of the Palladian villas is arranged in strict chronological order so as to present a complete view of works of this particular type that can confidently or conjecturally be attributed to Palladio. This is followed by a catalogue of the villas which are definitely by his hand and others attributed to him, those built in whole or in part, and those which exist only as designs or were built and then destroyed. These have not been divided into different groups but in each case the category to which one belongs is clearly indicated at the beginning of each entry.

The attribution of a villa is certain either because Palladio mentions it in the *Quattro Libri* or there exist designs or other documents demonstrating the fact. The choice of villas of uncertain attribution is based on the most recent catalogue, L. Puppi's fundamental *Andrea Palladio* (1973), with the addition of certain works suggested by convincing later studies.

The treatment of every villa contains an essential bibliography with no claim to completeness but which contains the most important or recent works on the subject. For the fuller treatment, the reader is referred to Puppi (1973). Whenever reference is made to unpublished documents, the details are given in the text. At the start of each entry there is practical information on how to reach the villa, its former site, or the site it was meant to occupy, together with opening hours (which may change to suit the owners' convenience).

Villa Godi

Lonedo di Lugo Vicentino (Vicenza), c. 1537; attribution certain.

From Vicenza to Thiene take state highway no. 349; then continue to Zugliano and Lugo. Lonedo lies above the town and the villa is clearly signposted and easy to find. Visits: Tuesday, Saturday, Sunday and other holidays, 19 March-31 May, 2 p.m.-6 p.m.; 1 June-31 August, 3 p.m.-7 p.m.; 1 September- 31 October, 2 p.m.-6 p.m. Parties of over ten people can arrange visits outside these hours: phone for a booking (tel. 0445/860561).

Traditionally held to be the earliest identifiable work of Palladio, the Villa Godi strikes the visitor at first sight both by its fine position on the hillside, dominating the River Astico, and the austerity of its structure, very different from the stereotyped image of a Palladian villa with pediment and columns.

The sturdy, rectangular building stands out from two asymmetrical lower wings; it consists of two equal blocks linked by a middle section whose front elevation is set back somewhat, to make room for a staircase leading up to the loggia, and also projects behind the building.

The *piano nobile* is enhanced by a Venetian window or *serliana*. In the plan, this middle axis, composed of the porticoed atrium of the salon, separates two identical sets of apartments each containing four rooms. The smooth outer surfaces are broken up only by the simple windows of the three storeys, and the arches of the loggias rest directly on pillars without bases or capitals.

The villa appears in plan and elevation in the second of Palladio's *Quattro Libri dell'Architettura*, hence there is no doubt of the attribution. The illustration presents some important differences from the completed building: the windows are given a more emphatic arrangement and vary in number; the central composition of the elevation is handled more decisively thanks to the staircase, which is made to comprise all three of the arches of the loggia and not just the central one as in the completed building, and it thrusts up higher above the wings. To these should be added the complex sequence of courtyards and porticoed outhouses surrounding the residential villa which forms the core. This is a good example of the way the illustrations in the *Quattro Libri* are reworkings of the original designs for didactic purposes and not reliable evidence of the architect's initial intentions. This drawing is a case in point: the arrangement of the outbuildings to the right would have been completely unfeasible in reality because of the way the ground falls sharply away on the site.

The biggest question mark hanging over Villa Godi is the exact chronology of its construction, as well as the phases and extent of Palladio's contribution. In all probability the project was entrusted to the *bottega* of the master builders of Pedemuro by the wealthy and powerful Godi family of Vicenza. They had already commissioned other work from the same builder: the portal of the church of the Servi and the funerary chapel in San Michele in Vicenza, subsequently destroyed. The scholars tend to attribute the major part of both these works to the youthful Andrea (not yet dubbed "Palladio") who had been working in the *bottega* since 1524, when he fled from his native Padua. Then, through natural talent and the teachings of the humanist and man of letters Giangiorgio Trissino, he gradually achieved, from the later 1530s on, an increasingly important role as architectural expert. He must have been responsible for the design of the new "manor house," part of a much broader plan to improve the property at Lonedo which had begun with the farm buildings in 1533, the date carved on the portico of the outhouse which still stands to the left of the villa.

The date when construction got under way can reasonably be put at about 1537, when Enrico Antonio Godi died and his son Girolamo took over the estate. Palladio says that the design was commissioned by Girolamo, who proclaims this fact in the inscription carved over the central arch of the loggia. The building was complete and fit for habitation by 1542, as shown by a statement made for the property register as well as a date on the façade. But the magnificent frescoes covering all the rooms of the *piano nobile* and one on the ground floor were painted later by Gualtiero Padovano, Giambattista Zelotti and Battista del Moro, as Palladio himself informs us in the treatise.

There has been great debate and speculation over Palladio's supposed dislike of this kind of decoration, which purportedly disturbs the limpid interiors of his buildings. Scholars like to cite his "hostile silence" over the frescoes by Paolo Veronese in the Villa Barbaro at Maser. In reality, what we know about the Villa Godi now undermines this thesis, since it is certain that Palladio himself prepared the rooms for the frescoes, and even arranged the layout for them between 1549 and 1552. This is proved by an autograph drawing from 1550 (published in Lewis, 1981, pp. 154-156) reproducing the wall of the central chamber towards the loggia, with the *trompe l'oeil* architecture and the arrangement of the various figures, trophies, festoons and cornices that were meant to be painted on it. At the same time Palladio closed up the thermal window towards the garden and replaced it with the present *serliana* or venetian window, probably more effective in illuminating the decoration.

Gualtiero Padovano, a member of the Paduan school, came to Lonedo in 1550, when he was at the height of his career. He and his *atelier* are responsible for the frescoes in the right wing, rich in symbols that are esoteric and at times indecipherable, in sharp, dry colours. They began from the loggia, where herms and monochrome grotesques give way in the vault to a central octagon with *Mercury and Spring*. A curious detail is the presence among the grotesques of little caricatures of flagellant friars, which some scholars have related to the client's Calvinist sympathies, also hinted at in the inscription over the main doorway: PROCUL ITE PROFANI ("Keep far hence, you profane!"). The first room is known as the "Chamber of the Putto" after

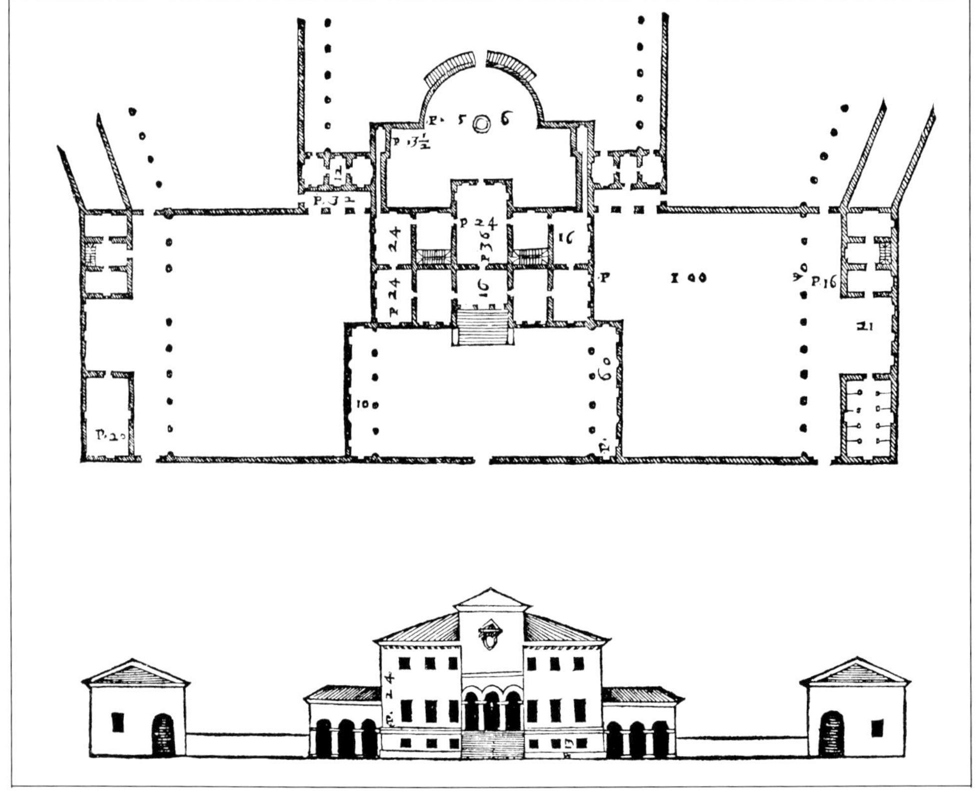

Drawing of plan and elevation of the Villa Godi (from the "Quattro Libri").

Villa Godi, front elevation.

the child painted at a window which opens onto a river landscape. Elegant monochrome female figures appear between the columns, with above them a frieze with divinities. Equally refined are the landscapes in the next chamber, the "Chamber of the Caesars," which seem to foreshadow Veronese's frescoes at the Villa Maser. They stretch away over the great arches scanned by Corinthian columns bearing a sumptuous frieze. The paintings in the next chamber, the "Chamber of Triumphs," are much more monotonous: its name comes from the subject of the frieze running under the ceiling. It is decorated with caryatids and a huge, dull landscape with the Colossus of Rhodes. There is also painting of a gentleman emerging from a *trompe l'oeil* door. The ceiling with *Virtue Chaining Vice* and other panels is attributed to Zelotti. The fourth chamber, next to the great hall, contains monochrome figures within architectural frames, and has suffered from nineteenth century restoration. Gualtiero Padovano died in about 1552-1553, leaving the decoration unfinished; it was completed by Giambattista Zelotti *circa* 1560 (documents show he was at the Villa Godi in 1561), assisted by Battista del Moro. Zelotti was coeval with and a fellow-student of Veronese, with whom he worked on Sanmichele's Villa Soranza at Treville (later demolished), where the frescoes illustrate some of the great themes of Mannerist art with the expected refinement of colouring, based on clear, limpid shades. The walls and ceilings of the hall are divided up by the complex architectural scheme devised by Palladio, with Corinthian columns and pilasters supporting arches and pediments. The paintings within this framework represent the two great battles be-

Villa Godi, Chamber of the Muses, fresco by Battista del Moro.

tween Darius and Alexander, on the two longer walls, while the wall with the main entrance represents *Hercules at the Crossroads*, flanked by triumphs; above the *serliana* on the wall opposite is a fresco of Fame with figures of prisoners. Women in colourful clothes lean over the trabeation, while *trompe l'oeil* windows open onto landscapes. The room to the left of the great hall, known as the "Chamber of the Arts,"contains niches with fine monochrome depictions of Spring and Summer, which are among the best in the cycle, and a landscape seen through an illusionist window framed by trophies and *putti*. There are also busts of emperors and other monochrome allegorical figures set in niches. The following chamber is divided up by columns bearing a splendid trabeation: the decoration is less coherent, partly due to the intervention of Battista del Moro, to whom is ascribed the painting of Nisus and Euryalus. Over the fireplace, a beautiful Venus listens

to Cupid, with Vulcan in the background and other divinities in the remaining panels. The Virtues appear over the doors, in poses somewhat lacking in spontaneity. The decoration of the other corner room is much more imaginative: in the sky above the massive ruins of a Greek temple hover the divinities of Olympus, the most conspicuous being the great nude of Venus. An equally effective piece is the painting over the mantelpiece, which shows a giant viewed from behind as he hurtles earthwards. The room to the left of the loggia, divided by up refined caryatids bearing a rich trabeation, is the work of Battista del Moro, a Veronese painter. His graceful style appears in the panels of *Muses and Poets*. The "Chamber of the Seasons," on the ground floor, painted by Zelotti, contains his favoured motifs: *trompe l'oeil* statues, female figures, and prisoners cover the walls, together with a landscape. The centre of the vault is decorated with an oval, supported by imposing caryatids, framing an allegory of *Virtue Banishing Vice*.

The last trace of Palladio ascertained at Lonedo is the semicircular design of the rear court; at its centre stands the beautiful wellhead, carved from a single block of stone and bearing the date 1555. In the later 1570s the right wing was built: it is set slightly back from the main line of the building, and its exaggerated length upsets the balance of Palladio's loggia opposite, with its three arches. The building has not been tampered with to any extent since then: in the seventeenth century the service rooms were added at the back and the forecourt was redesigned, following a change in the course of the main road, which used to run parallel with the façade and not far from it. (The various stages of construction are described in a series of charts published by Kubelik, 1974, pp. 457-458 and Puppi, 1974, pp. 98-99.)

What else is there to say about this early work by Palladio. It marks the first stage in Palladio's quest to create a new type of country house for the upper classes; in this respect it exactly parallels the virtually contemporary work of Jacopo Sansovino at the Villa Garzoni at Pontecasale and Michele Sanmicheli at the Villa Soranzana at Treville. The design of the Villa Godi drew on certain Quattrocento country houses, as appears in the juxtaposition of the two side blocks. Another important source was provided by the study of books on ancient Roman villas and drawings of ancient buildings, with the encouragement of Giangiorgio Trissino, who completed the renewal of his suburban villa at Cricoli, near Vicenza, in that same year (1537), superficially inspired by Raphael's design for the Villa Madama in Rome. Together with traditional motifs common in local buildings—the simple profile of the cornices or the aperture above the door leading into the salon—Palladio here experimented with the thermal window (derived from classical architecture and later replaced by the *serliana*), which he probably found in the drawings of Sangallo and recurs in his later work. The ground plan, laid out around a central axis, forming the loggia and the salon, also seems to foreshadow Palladio's later handling of space; while the gap which appears in the completed building between the main residence and the outbuildings reveals the tendency to separate the privileged sphere of the nobility from the humble world of labour, a break which Palladio only bridged later on by fusing the two into a functional and figurative whole.

Bibliography: Vasari, 1568, p. 528; Palladio, 1570, 1. II, p. 65; Muttoni, 1740, pp. 43 ff.; Bertotti Scamozzi, 1778, pp. 23-26; Magrini, 1845, pp. 8, 79, 237; Burger, 1909, pp. 16-25; Dalla Pozza, 1943-1963, p. 120; Pane, 1961, pp. 103 ff.; Crosato, 1962, pp. 120-126; Forssman, 1965, pp. 18-22; Ackerman, 1967, pp. 50-52; Ivanoff, 1967, p. 24, n. 21; Pallucchini, 1968, pp. 208-210; Hofer, 1969; Zorzi, 1969, pp. 21- 32; Barbieri, 1970, pp. 64-66; Cevese, 1971, I, pp. 80-97 and 1973, pp. 54-55; Puppi 1973, pp. 238-240 and 1974, pp. 98-99; Kubelik, 1974, pp. 457-458; Berger, 1978, pp. 30-42; Burns, 1979, p. 21; Battilotti, 1979-1980, pp. 211-212; Rigon, 1980, nos. 1-3; Lewis, 1981, pp. 154-156; Canova, 1985, pp. 70-79; Muraro, 1986, pp. 170-177; Bödefeld-Hinz, 1987, pp. 106-108; Costant, 1987, pp. 35- 36; Zaupa, 1989.

Villa Piovene

30 Lonedo di Lugo Vicentino (Vicenza), 1539-1540; attributed in part to Palladio.

The villa stands a few hundred yards from the Villa Godi (q.v.). Open for visits every day between 2 p.m. and 7 p.m.; in winter between 2 p.m. and 5 p.m.

Not far from the Villa Godi, further up the same hill at Lonedo, Villa Piovene at first sight looks much more "Palladian" than its celebrated and austere neighbour. It has an imposing hexastyle pronaos, with a double staircase leading up to it and two rectilinear porticoed wings stretching away on either side: all elements that are typical of Palladio's mature style. In fact down to the end of the eighteenth century there was the archivolt of an inner doorway (later mounted between the two flights of steps leading up to the loggia) bearing the inscription: ANDREUS PALLADIUS ARCHITECTUS. This has not prevented the attribution of the design—not included in the *Quattro Libri*—from being called in question because of its many incongruities, not all connected with the supposed constraints imposed by an earlier building. The solution to the problem lies in documentary evidence and analysis of its structures, which show how the present villa was built in various different stages, only the earliest being the work of Palladio.
The new manor house of the Piovene family is described as completed and fit for habitation in a cadastral record of 1541, but as appears from a law case in 1567 it was much smaller than now, the front elevation being approximately 21 metres long (instead of 35), a measurement that corresponds roughly to the seven vertical divisions of the central section. Its construction can be dated back to the years just before 1541, and so it must be closely related to the nearby Villa Godi. It is highly likely that it was the example of the Villa Godi (with finishing touches being put to the building in 1540) that awakened a desire to emulate it, especially when we remember the profound affinity of interests that linked these two noble families of Vicenza. The Villa Piovene retains the severe style and highly characteristic modillion cornice of the Villa Godi which can still be seen on the rear of the building, still largely intact. The front elevation must presumably have had a *serliana* of the type found in the Villa Forni at Montecchio Precalcino. Palladio's work at the Villa Piovene in all probability went no further. The enlargement of the residential section to its present dimensions and the insertion of the pronaos must belong to the period between the mid-1570s and 1587, the date carved on the pronaos. The banal layout of the inner spaces, the marked asymmetry of the façade, with the imbalance created by the space between the windows at the end of the façade and those coupled near the loggia, the crude way the colonnade is attached to the latter feature—all these cannot be attributed to Palladio but some anonymous imitator who used elements like the pronaos which had by then become common.
A map from the mid-seventeenth century (printed by Puppi, 1974) shows the villa still part of a system of outhouses, lean-tos, houses and pigeon lofts all inside an enclosure. The porticoed outbuilding already completed on the left shows, however, that yet another phase of construction was under way, to give greater rhetorical emphasis to the residential section. This process was completed in the middle years of the eighteenth century by Francesco Muttoni, a neo-Palladian architect. All the earlier elements were removed and the villa was left isolated at the end of the long, monumental flight of steps rising from the richly ornate entrance gate, flanked by numerous sculptures from the *bottega* of Orazio Marinali, a sculptor of Vicenza. Outside the villa's enclosure, by the service entrance, stands the family chapel of San Gerolamo, which bears the date 1496. Behind it stretches a fine park in the Romantic style from the early nineteenth century.

Bibliography: Muttoni, 1740, Index; Bertotti Scamozzi, 1778, pp. 27-28; Magrini, 1845, p. 287; Dalla Pozza, 1943-1963, pp. 124-125; Pane, 1961, p. 190; Ackerman, 1967, p. 52; Zorzi, 1969, pp. 204-208; Barbieri, 1970, p. 24; Cevese, 1971, II, pp. 459-460; Puppi, 1973, pp. 241-242 and 1974; Muraro, 1986, pp. 178-181; Costant, 1987, pp. 147-148.

Villa Piovene, front elevation.

Villa Valmarana

32 Vigardolo di Monticello
Conte Otto (Vicenza),
1541, attribution not certain.

From Vicenza take the state highway no. 53 for Treviso, turn left after a few kilometres to Monticello Conte Otto. After driving through the town of Monticello Conte Otto one comes to Vigardolo. In the centre of the village turn left to reach Via Vigardoletto 33, where the villa stands. Visits: Saturday, 3 p.m.-6 p.m., other days by request (tel. 0444/596242).

The scholars are divided over the attribution of this villa to Palladio, though there are sound reasons for placing it among his early works from the years around 1540. Features typical of this period are the severity of the markedly rectangular structure, the smoothness of the walls (as in the Villa Godi), and the way the Venetian window or *serliana* has been used to enliven the slightly projecting middle section of the front elevation, a motif that is repeated in the Palazzo Civena at Vicenza (1540) and in many of Palladio's youthful drawings. There is also the evidence of an autograph drawing by Palladio (London, R.I.B.A., XVII, 2) which can reasonably be interpreted as the design for the villa: the layout and form fit the building, as well as the measurements of the rooms, though the façade has undergone extensive changes in the course of construction. An attic storey has been inserted, the cornice of the lower windows has been radically simplified, the *serliana* in the middle is no longer set within an arch but has two oculi above the flanking windows, and above all it avoids the break in the façade created continuing the cornice as far as the projection in the middle. These discrepancies in the design and the awkward proportions in the façade can perhaps be attributed to work that was unsupervised by the architect and the fact—as is suggested by a study of the masonry—that there was already a building on the site to be reckoned with.
The villa was begun in 1541, a date given in a cadastral document which seems to imply that the work had not advanced greatly by the year's end. The owner was Giuseppe Valmarana, from a minor branch of one of the most powerful aristocratic families of Vicenza.
There are conflicting opinions about the sources Palladio drew on for this villa, especially in its design. Some scholars believe it was produced soon after his return from his sojourn in Rome in 1541, and hence influenced by his studies of ancient Roman baths; others point out that the use of the *serliana* precludes direct observation of Roman architecture and suggests instead that Palladio was influenced by the collection of designs by Sebastiano Serlio which was widely known in the Veneto from the third decade of the sixteenth century on. There are also appreciable signs of a knowledge of Giulio Romano and the Palazzo del Te in Mantua, especially in the rusticated columns supporting the pediments of the windows shown in the drawings; these were never built but clearly have affinities with the Palazzo Thiene in Vicenza. Palladio in these years was trying to define a new type of aristocratic rural mansion, and with this in mind he laid out the ground plan of the Villa Valmarana on a T-shaped central axis linking front and back to provide a suitable arrangement of the smaller rooms, a pattern that even at this early date looks confident and afforded scope for future developments. It should also be remembered that Palladio had intended his first, timid hint at a pediment (unfortunately not executed) for this villa, transferring a feature of sacred architecture to a secular building with a celebratory function.
Two maps of the Venetian Magistrature for *Beni Inculti* (published by Kubelik, 1974, pp. 452-453), dated 1597 and 1607, show the villa with a large enclosed forecourt and bounded on the right by a fishpond. They also show that in the decade between the two maps a long rustic portico was built to the right of the main residential block, terminating in a dovecote, both of which no longer exist.
The Villa Valmarana used to be completely covered with frescoes. All that remain are two Cinquecento medallions in the centre of the ceiling of the two small rooms in the short wing on the left, depicting the *Presentation to the Temple* and the *Allegory of Aurora*. They have been ascribed to Alessandro Maganza of Vicenza. The badly damaged decoration of the atrium, framed by columns and

Original design for the Villa Valmarana at Vigardolo (London, R.I.B.A., XVII, 2).

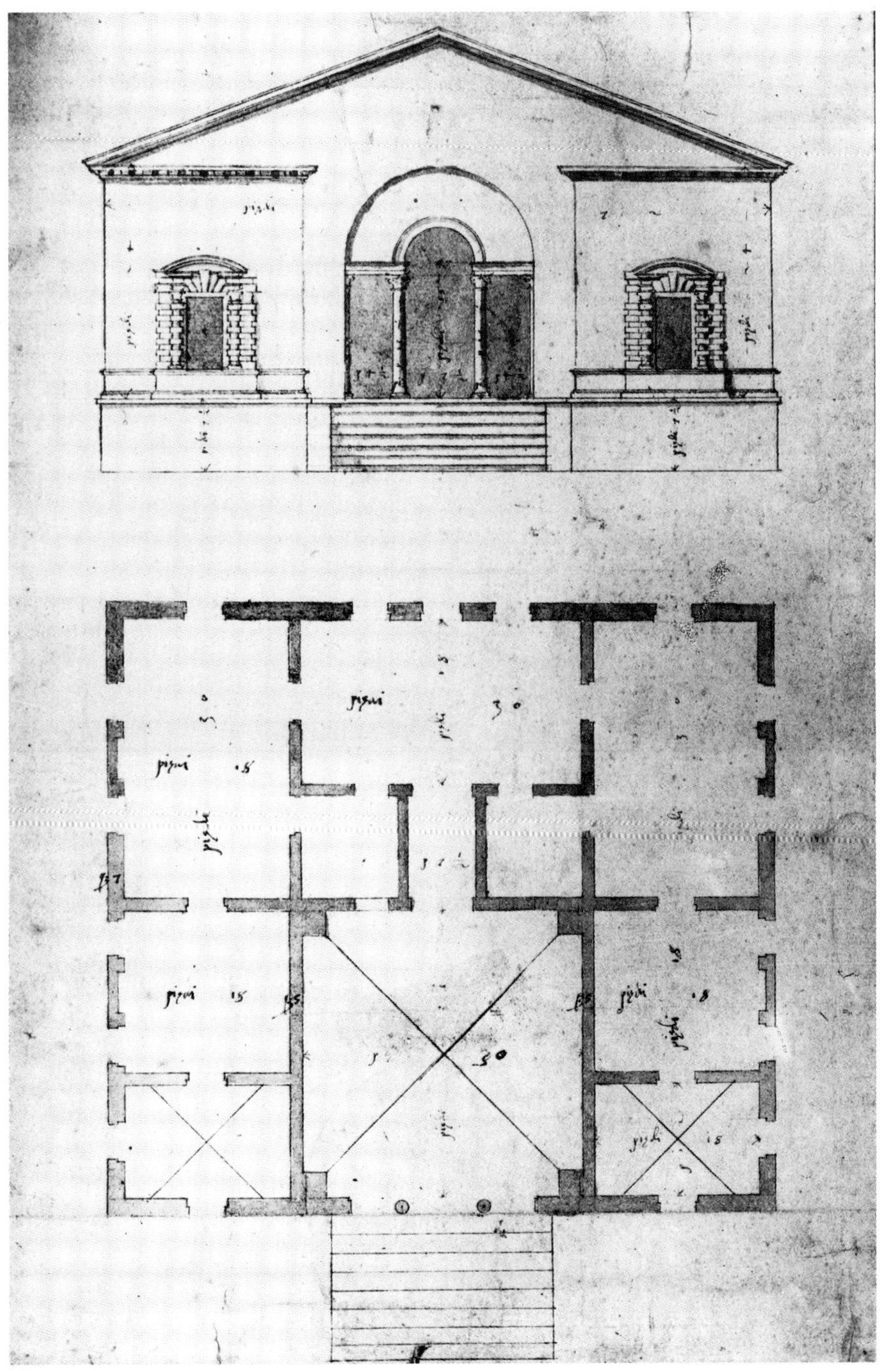

Villa Valmarana (Vigardolo), front elevation.

ornamented with monochrome figures, seems to have been executed by some unknown painter of the eighteenth century. The frieze in the salon with the *Stories of Joseph the Jew* and perhaps also the hunting scenes in the next room are outstanding works, executed by Costantino Pasqualotto in the eighteenth century.

The villa has been recently restored.

Bibliography: Crosato, 1962, pp. 210-211; Dalla Pozza, 1964-1965, pp. 229-238; Zorzi, 1969, pp. 60-62; Barbieri, 1970, pp. 67-68; Cevese, 1971, II, pp. 506-507 and 1973, pp. 51-53; Puppi, 1973, pp. 245-247 and 1974; Kubelik, 1974, pp. 452-453; Burns, 1975, p. 182; Lewis, 1981, p. 72; Costant, 1987, p. 40.

Villa Forni, front elevation.

Montecchio Precalcino (Vicenza),
1541-1542 (?); attribution not certain.

From Vicenza take the road for Bassano as far as the bridge over the Astico at Passo di Riva. Then turn left towards Montecchio Precalcino, skirting the embankment. At the bend turn left for Via Cerato 7, just after the crossroads, where the villa stands.

This delightful little villa, which is not included in the *Quattro Libri*, has always been surrounded by energetic debate, with Palladian scholars divided over the question of whether it is by Palladio or not. Its history is still shrouded in uncertainty and this also helps kindle controversy.
All that can definitely be said is that it was left to the Cerato family, in 1610, in the will of the merchant, painter and antiquarian Girolamo Forni of Vicenza. Those who suppose that this myriad-minded character was also the original client are forced to suggest a late date for construction since Cerato was born in about 1530. Some scholars even date it to the later 1570s and attribute it to Alessandro

Vittoria, a sculptor from Trentino, who worked in Vicenza in 1576-1577 and was a close friend of Forni. He may also be responsible for the decoration of the villa: the pediment bears a coat of arms supported by two Winged Victories and the four bas-reliefs of the Seasons which used to stand over the loggia apertures. (They can be seen in seventeenth and eighteenth century engravings of the villa, but were removed in the 1920s and replaced by a copy of the coat of arms and two reliefs of fluvial divinities, so all that remains of the original external decoration is the mask on the loggia arch.)

Other scholars, inclined to favour Palladio, have suggested a date around the 1560s. It is suggested that the panel window sills used at Montecchio are characteristic of this period (as at the Palazzo Valmarana in Vicenza or the refectory of San Giorgio Maggiore in Venice), and they point out the affinities between this villa and the façade of the house of the notary Piero Cogollo in Vicenza.

Then there is a third approach to the problem, a wholehearted acceptance of this work as by Palladio, with the design and construction dated to the early 1540s. This would mean that the client could not have been Girolamo Forni but someone else, whose identity has not been definitely established, though recent research in the archives seems to point to Antonio Brandizio, a nobleman who belonged to the circle of friends close to Palladio and invested in land in the *contrada* of Capo di Sotto, the very area where the villa stands. This theory appears convincing because the villa, in its extreme simplicity, achieves a remarkable clarity and balance in its composition, and in many respects is closely related to the villas designed or built in Palladio's early period. The sparing use of classical elements, the division of the elevation into three sections, the small attic windows, the modillions on the cornice, are all highly suggestive of the Villa Godi; the cornices on the windows of the *piano nobile* recur in the Villa Gazzotti at Bertesina; while the *serliana* motif, recurrent in designs from the 1540s, is used at Montecchio with almost geometrical rigour and precision in the loggia of the pronaos. Originally the *serliana* would be repeated on the rear of the building, at the end of the salon, so creating a perfect rapport between the two elevations while also achieving that ideal interpenetration between the interior of the house and the surrounding countryside that reappears in Palladio's finest villas.

The insertion of the decorative features on the façade, however, must have been due to Girolamo Forni, after the villa changed hands, and in this respect Alessandro Vittoria may also have come to work on it. But the very fine stucco busts over the three doors of the central chamber suggest the style of the sculptor Bartolomeo Ridolfi, and the two mantelpieces from the late Cinquecento which originally stood in the two corner rooms at the front of the building are also outstanding work. (That in the right-hand room has now been moved to the ground floor.)

Bibliography: Muttoni, 1740, Index; Bertotti Scamozzi, 1778, p. 44; Pane, 1961, pp. 104-105; Ackerman, 1967, pp. 59-60; Zorzi, 1969, pp. 230-231; Cevese, 1971, II, pp. 486-487; Puppi, 1973, pp. 247-248; Burns, 1975, pp. 202-203 and 1979, pp. 14-15; Costant, 1987, pp. 126-127; Zaupa, 1989.

Villa Gazzotti Grimani

Bertesina (Vicenza)
1542 (?); attribution certain.

The villa stands in the suburb of Bertesina, to the east of Vicenza, in Via San Cristoforo 23, to the left of the parish church.

Palladio's claims to the design of the villa are based on a set of autograph drawings which show the course of the project. The building has a rectangular plan and develops on a single storey along a long façade, marked off by composite pilasters which divide it into seven bays. The central bay, with access provided by a short flight of steps of recent construction, comprises three arches (as at the Villa Godi) leading into the portico and emphasized by the pediment. In each of the four intercolumnar spaces on either side there is a window with a tympanum.
An examination of the masonry and the presence of a window and door on the east front suggest that part of an earlier thirteenth-fourteenth century building have been incorporated into the villa. Other clues, like the way the ends of the elevation seem to break off sharply, the unfinished state of the sides, and the incongruous simplification of the roof, as well as the evidence provided by the drawings, lead one to suppose that the present building is the result of the reduction of a scheme (or perhaps what was only meant to be its momentary suspension) which was far more ambitious and far-reaching.

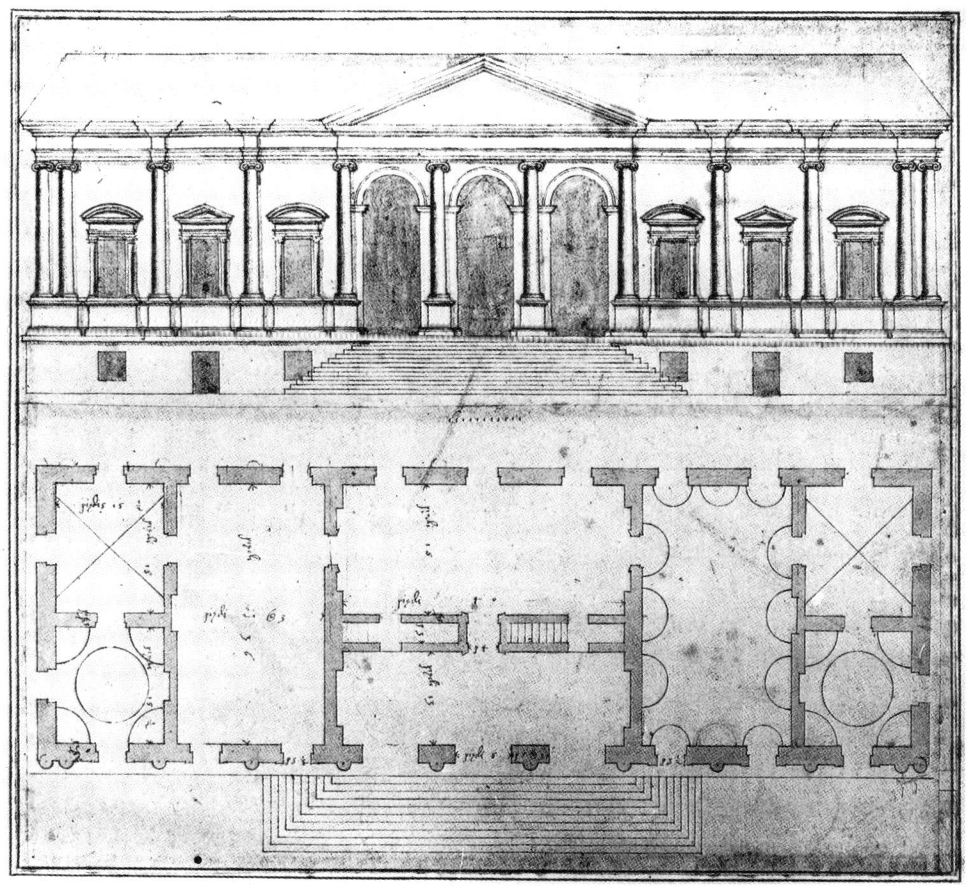

Study for the plan and elevation of the Villa Gazzotti Grimani (London, R.I.B.A., XVII, 27).

Villa Gazzotti Grimani, view of the whole.

First we should follow the phases of its construction. The villa is one of the few private buildings by Palladio not commissioned by a nobleman. The owner was the salt-dealer Taddeo Gazzotti. Scholars agree in setting the date of its conception at the start of the 1540s, partly for stylistic reasons and partly because that was the beginning of an unfortunately short-lived period of great prosperity in the life of the merchant.

It must be said that recent research has discovered that the youthful Andrea di Pietro was living in the merchant's house as early as 1534. The theory that the future Palladio, even at this early date, might have been engaged in devising a design for the house is very tempting, even calling in question the previous studies of his early work. But until further research has been completed, it is advisable to see the date as testifying to a lengthy acquaintance between the two figures. Be that as it may, the construction of the new villa went forward slowly, then came to a complete halt with Gazzotti's financial setbacks, soon leading to bankruptcy, so that in 1549 the Republic of Venice sought to recover his debts by confiscating the house and putting it up for auction, describing it as unfinished. It was then completed by the new owner, Girolamo Grimani, following his purchase of the property in 1550.

These two stages in its construction emerge clearly from the study of the building made in the eighteenth century by Ottavio Bertotti Scamozzi, before the interior was modified (only the loggia and the central cruciform chamber are original). Initially only the portico with the two side rooms and the staircase were built, then the rear section was added, together with the unfortunate projecting part, clearly foreign to Palladio's intentions and perhaps the work of Grimani. The measurements and layout of the rooms correspond exactly to one of the autograph designs mentioned above (London, R.I.B.A., XVI, 16A), which can be taken as the drawing used to plan the layout of the present building. The latter is nothing more (to return to the observations made at the start of this entry) than the reduction of a more ambitious programme, likewise substantiated by the other drawings in the archives; the most significant of these drawings (London, R.I.B.A., XVII, 27) shows the same frontal scheme as in the completed building, but it provides for one more intercolumnar space per side and Ionic columns instead of composite pilasters. In the other drawings (London, R.I.B.A., XVI, 18 and 16B, C) the ground plan covers an area twice as large. It is reasonable to conclude that when construction began, the plan seemed too ambitious and costly for the finances of Gazzotti, though he was still comfortably off, and so a scaled-down version which ensured an effective image was decided on, shelving the initial project until a later date.

The Villa Gazzotti, taken together with the set of related drawings, constitutes a further step in the development of Palladio's architectural vocabulary. From the closed form of the Villa Godi he moved on to a new dialectic between architectural space and the open countryside here at Bertesina, together with a clear interest in the work of Bramante and Raphael, which he had studied in Rome in 1541. All the same, the main influence at this period is Giulio Romano, and the central feature of the villa—closely reminiscent of the upper arches of the Palazzo Thiene in Vicenza—seems to have been influenced by a journey Palladio apparently made to Mantua late in 1542, accompanying Giulio Romano on a trip to study the loggias of the Basilica in Vicenza. There is also a marked similarity between the dentellation of the base of the pediment and the elevation facing the garden at the Villa Madama in Rome.

Bibliography: Bertotti Scamozzi, 1778, pp. 56-57; Magrini, 1845, pp. 289-290; Dalla Pozza, 1943-1963 pp. 106-118; Pane, 1961, pp. 101-102; Forssman, 1965, pp. 22-26; Ackerman, 1967, p. 41; Zorzi, 1969, pp. 67-70; Barbieri, 1970, pp. 68-69; Cevese, 1971, II, p. 653 and 1973, pp. 53-54; Puppi, 1973, pp. 250-251; Fairbairn, in Burns, 1975, pp. 182-185; Berger, 1978, pp. 109-115; Lewis, 1981, pp. 72-76; Canova, 1985, pp. 80-85; Bödefeld-Hinz, 1987, pp. 110-111; Costant, 1987, p. 43; Zaupa, 1989.

Villa Pisani

40 Bagnolo di Lonigo (Vicenza),
1542 and c. 1561; attribution certain.

From Vicenza follow the road to Verona as far as Alte Ceccato, then turn left and after passing through Lonigo take the road towards Cologna Veneta, which soon reaches Bagnolo. The villa stands on the right, beyond the embankment of the River Guà. It can be visited on Wednesdays and Fridays, 9 a.m.-11 a.m., 2 p.m.-6.30 p.m. Other days by telephone booking (tel. 0444/831104).

It is always saddening to see a building that has suffered the ravages of time and been disfigured by man, especially when one knows its history and something of its ancient splendour. This sorrow is softened in the case of the Villa Pisani by the excellent restoration work that has recently been completed and revived the building's inherent dignity, despite the injuries inflicted on it through the centuries. The villa appears as a square structure made up of two distinct blocks. That to the north-west is larger and deeper, and faces the courtyard and countryside with its clear, luminous façade, with a thermal window in the middle section that has finally been re-opened. The block facing it lies between turrets that suggest a Quattrocento villa-castle, and is animated by the intense chiaroscuro of the rustication of the three-arched loggia, inscribed within the Doric order of the pilasters and surmounted by a pediment. This must once have been the most important side, facing the River Guà, which was navigable and formed the main line of communication with Venice. Now the river is blocked not far from here by the embankment built in the nineteenth century to control flooding. Above the tall plinth, where the striking rusticated ashlar work marks the corners of the villa and frames the basement windows, rise the slender windows of the *piano nobile*, with its simple, elegant cornice, and above this runs a row of square attic windows. The recent restorations (to mention only its more evident aspects) have cleared away the earth that covered up most of the plinth, restored the apertures of the windows on the *piano nobile* to their full size, level with the perimeter of the cornices (they had been narrowed on the inside), and renewed the bi-apsidal space of the loggia, which had been divided up by partitions while the side arches had been bricked in. Work was also carried out on the interior, which had been marred by nineteenth century conversions: the T-shaped central chamber, which links the loggia and the entrance from the courtyard, has reacquired its true brightness thanks to the re-opening of the thermal window in the façade. It has also been freed from an incongruous gallery running along the opposite wall, under the second thermal window, while the latter had also been bricked up since Palladio's time because of the construction of the pediment above the loggia.

The frescoes that survive in the cross barrel-vaulting in the salon—also restored—are attributed to Bernardino India of Verona. The muscular figures in the panels of the barrel vaulting (the central one depicts *Phaeton in the Chariot of the Sun*) recall the paintings in the Chamber of the Emperors at the Villa Poiana at Pojana Maggiore. The south-east room, under the turret, is also frescoed with cycles on different subjects by an unknown painter of the Cinquecento.

The attribution of the villa to Palladio is certain. Palladio himself published its plan and elevation in the *Quattro Libri*, and Vasari mentions it as Palladio's work in the 1568 edition of the *Lives of the Painters*. The various stages of design and construction have proved difficult to reconstruct, though now there is fairly general agreement among scholars on the main sequence of events.

The villa was commissioned by the three brothers Vittore, Marco and Daniele Pisani, Venetian patricians, and was planned as the central point of their vast estates at Bagnolo which their father Giovanni had purchased from 1523 on from the Venetian treasury. Work immediately began on extensive reclamation and drainage projects to prevent the floods that used to be frequent. This property, which had earlier been confiscated by the Republic from the Counts of Nogarola, guilty of rebellion during the War of the League of Cambrai, comprised outhouses, mills and the old manor house. The latter was built in the fourteenth century inside the ancient mediaeval castle of Bagnolo, whose ruins can still be seen to the south of the villa. It is not

Drawing with plan and elevation of the Villa Pisani at Bagnolo (from the "Quattro Libri").

known whether the new villa was built on the site of the former palace of the Nogarola family, but it was definitely a completely new structure, apparently built in two distinct stages. Two declarations to the Venetian treasury by the Pisani brothers show that construction started after 1540, when there was no mention of a manor house at Bagnolo, and was partially completed by 1545, when the documents mention "a newly built palace." This date is confirmed by the inscription 1544 still clearly visible in a fresco in the villa in the first half of the nineteenth century, and also by thermoluminescent testing, though confined to the part of the building facing onto the courtyard.
The loggia towards the river must be at least about fifteen years later, but must have been executed before 1562, when it appears clearly marked on a map belonging to the family (see Puppi, 1973, p. 340). The date 1567 which the German scholar Burger saw carved over the loggia at the beginning of the twentieth century is something of a mystery, as well as the cause of this lag in the construction of what must have been the main façade of the building. Be that as it may, it resulted in a conspicuous alteration to the original plan. The way the design was worked out appears in a set of autograph drawings by Palladio which clearly refer to the Villa Pisani (London, R.I.B.A., XVI, 16, 18 and XVII, 27). They allow us to retrace the development of a steadily more coherent ground plan which finally leads to what must have been the final design (XVII, 27) of the central T-shaped chamber.

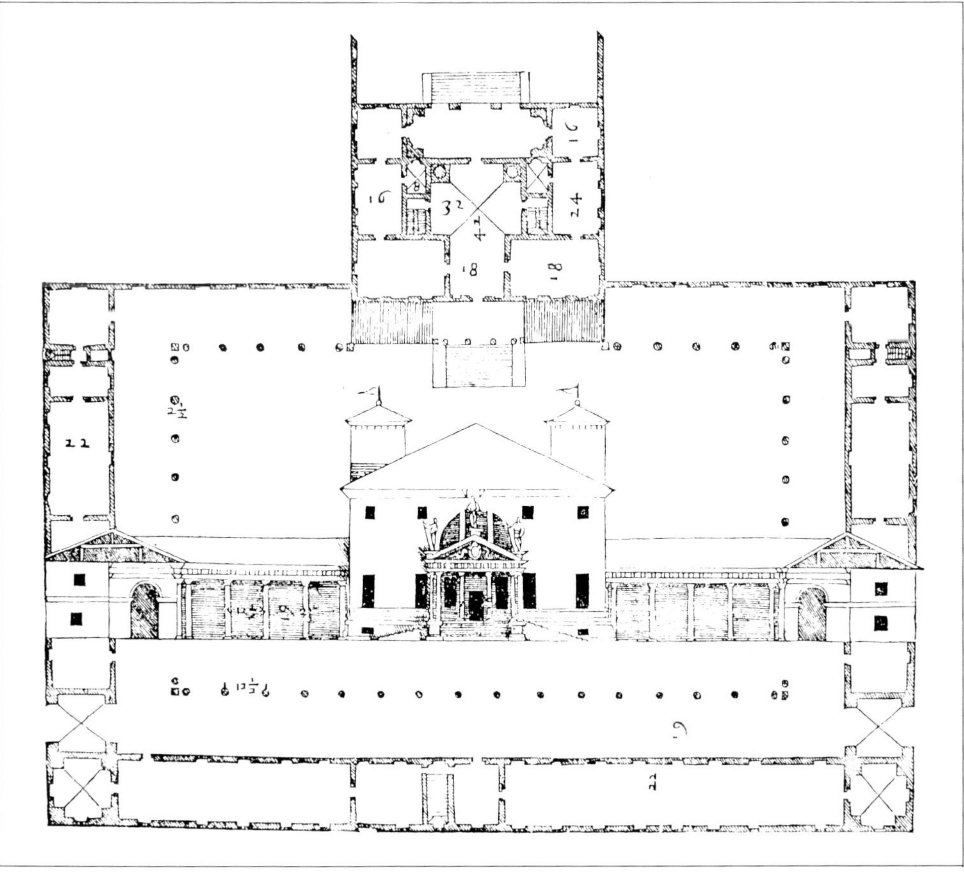

Villa Pisani (Bagnolo), elevation towards the River Guà and elevation towards the countryside.

As for the side towards the river, Palladio never departed from the concept of a semicircular colonnade, handled in a range of different forms in the drawings. This motif is clearly derivative from the Belvedere built by Donato Bramante in the Vatican (now destroyed); the numerous drawings he made of it suggest that he had seen it for himself during his stay in Rome in 1541. But as I have said, the recess was abandoned during construction and replaced by the present three-arched loggia, which is shallower and so called for the addition of a short terminal arm to the cross-shaped chamber of the salon and closure of the thermal window above, masked on the outside by the pediment.

In this second phase of construction a rustic colonnade was built, terminating in two tall dovecotes, all undoubtedly Palladio's own design. Unfortunately they had been destroyed by the early seventeenth century, but the 1562 map shows them clearly in front of the residential block, and Vasari admired them during his trip to the Veneto in 1566, when he saw "this great and splendid courtyard of the Doric order, with fine columns." (The present outhouse on the west side is neoclassical work, perhaps from the early nineteenth century.) Immediately afterwards—by 1569, the date of the map that depicts it (see Puppi, 1973, p. 340)—another outhouse was built: it was arranged as three sides of a large rectangle, on the other side of the road, adjoining the Pisani's rice-fields. This building was—in a manner of speaking—more fortunate than the annex to the main residence: it was struck by lightning in the early nineteenth century, rebuilt, bombed in an air raid on the second-last day of World War II, and the west side then rebuilt; and in this way it has come down to us now. It is almost unanimously attributed to Palladio because of the elegance of the great Tuscan columns, though some doubts hang over the main doorway with its rusticated stonework.

Villa Pisani is of great interest, apart from the remarkable stylistic quality of the final result, because the vicissitudes of its construction show how Palladio went about his work, by degrees, without a rigid plan, adapting it to changing circumstances or requirements. This is at the opposite pole from the fixed abstractions which seem to be suggested by the *Quattro Libri*. In this case the design in the treatise diverges in numerous ways from the building itself, and seems to have been subordinated to the abstract needs of the layout of the page—for example the way the courtyard is always represented as lying in front of the mansion—rather than any intention of offering a correct interpretation of the complex. This is the only way we can explain the fact that the treatise shows us the villa from the more modest side, facing the courtyard, but "ennobled" by Palladio for the occasion with the not particularly felicitous addition of a pronaos below the thermal window, which was never envisaged for the building. Similarly, for reasons of space, the courtyard is shown as wholly surrounded by porticoes and is markedly foreshortened.

Bibliography: Vasari, 1568, p. 528; Palladio, 1570, 1. II, p. 47; Muttoni, 1740, p. 21; Bertotti Scamozzi, 1778, pp. 14-17; Magrini, 1845, pp. 79, 241; Burger, 1909, pp. 40-47; Pane, 1961, pp. 224-225; Dalla Pozza, 1964-1965, pp. 203- 216; Ackerman, 1967, pp. 38-40; Zorzi, 1969, pp. 52-60; Barbieri, 1970, pp. 70-72; Cevese, 1971, I, pp. 100-109 and 1973, pp. 55-56; Puppi, 1973, pp. 254-257; Kubelik, 1974, pp. 447-449; Berger, 1978, pp. 103-108; Pereswiet-Soltan, 1978; Goedicke-Slusallek-Kubelik, 1980, pp. 106-112; Rigon, 1980, no. 4; Lewis, 1981, pp. 81-87; Muraro, 1981-1982 and 1986, pp. 182-185; Canova, 1985, pp. 86-93; Bödefeld-Hinz, 1987, pp. 108-109; Costant, 1987, pp. 45-46.

Villa Muzani, known as "La Pisa"

44 Malo (Vicenza)
early 1540s;
attribution not certain, now destroyed.

The villa used to stand on the edge of Malo, in the locality called Pisa, on the right of state highway no. 46 as you arrive from Vicenza making for Schio, on the edge of the built-up area. The site is marked by the remains of the front of the boundary wall and the private chapel.

The villa was destroyed in 1919 when a store of ammunition left from World War I exploded. All we have are some photographs and a survey of the ground plan from the nineteenth century (see Zorzi, 1969, f. 403-404). A great staircase led up to the front elevation, terminated by two corner turrets, a common feature of Quattrocento villas. In the middle there was a loggia with three slender arches surmounted by a tympanum. All the windows were sharp-edged, that is without mouldings. At the sides of the main residence, and set back slightly from it, there were two wings containing the outbuildings, with five arches and barn-space set above them.
The villa does not appear in the *Quattro Libri* and the attribution to Palladio is much debated: it rests on what is necessarily a superficial appraisal of the old photos and a court case of 1559, in which Palladio was called on to decide the payment due to a workman, Giorgio da Rigollo of Campione, for construction of the loggias and dovecotes. This document has lent itself to different interpretations. Some scholars see it as the start of construction, commissioned by Troilo Muzani, a nobleman of Vicenza. Others hold that Palladio's role as arbitrator means that he was not involved in the design of the villa, and attribute it to a master builder and imitator of his style, Pietro da Nanto, who was engaged in the same year and with the same workmen in building another villa for Troilo's brother Claudio at Rettorgole di Caldogno, now lost and also attributed, though with less support, to Palladio. The most plausible theory is probably that only the main residence of the Villa Muzani was designed by Palladio, in the early 1540s, while some other master builder—who could well have been Pietro da Nanto—was probably responsible for the two porticoed wings mentioned in the 1559 document, which seem from the photos not to be Palladian in style. If this theory is accepted, then the early dating of the building would be more likely, while the use of turrets, the clean surfaces, the solid fascia on which the arches are set, the *serliana* planned for the rear elevation at the end of the central axis, and the poverty of the classical vocabulary, are all features common to the early works, from the Villas Godi and Forni to the Villa Pisani at Bagnolo.

Bibliography: Dalla Pozza, 1943, pp. 182-189; Pane, 1961, pp. 213-214; Ackerman, 1967, p. 76; Barbieri, 1967; Zorzi, 1969, pp. 222-223; Puppi, 1973, p. 258; Zaupa, 1989.

Villa Pagliarino

Lanzè (Vicenza),
before 1545; design never built.

Lanzè can be easily reached from the road between Vicenza and Treviso: turn right a few kilometres after Lisiera.

We know of this design by Palladio for a villa for Bartolomeo Pagliarino, a nobleman of Vicenza, from a copy of one of his drawings made by an unknown collaborator to be sent to the client, at that time living in Venice. At first the drawing (London, R.I.B.A., XVI, 3) was connected with Palladio's design for the Villa Poiana at Pojana Maggiore because of the misinterpretation of the client's name on the back of the sheet as well as the identical layout of the plan of the main residence, with a T-shaped salon in both buildings. Other points of similarity are the location of the inner staircases, the fireplaces, the shape and proportions of the rooms. But the Pagliarino design has a portico screened by a *serliana* and crowned—conjecturally—by a tympanum, and projects from the line of the façade. Access is provided by two lateral staircases set against the sides of the building, a motif derived from the temple of Clitumnus which also appears in one of the drawings believed to be a preparatory sketch for the Villa Pisani at Bagnolo: it was later built, on a much more imposing scale, at the Villa Foscari at the Malcontenta.
Bartolomeo Pagliarino was a close friend of other clients of Palladio, especially Girolamo Godi (Archivio di Stato di Vicenza, Notarile Alvise Dalle Ore, b. 6965, dated 19 July 1561) and had married a cousin of Iseppo Porto, the client who commissioned the famous palace in *contrà* Porti di Vicenza. He possessed immense estates at Lanzè, clearly marked on a map of 1623 (published in Burns, 1979 [II], pp. 116-119) and this confirms the location earmarked for the villa. Palladio's design is perfectly adapted to the shape of the property, which lay between two roads and faced the town square, and was washed for a short stretch by a watercourse on the right. The villa was conceived as a series of closed courts; the great forecourt, reserved for the outhouses but "ennobled" by loggias and a porticoed entrance, was followed by a second court with the manorial residence, with others set at the sides, finally reaching the court that stretched down to the stream.
The death of his client in 1545 (Archivio di Stato di Vicenza, Notarile Alvise Dalle Ore, b. 6965, 19 July 1561) was in all probability the reason why the villa was never built, and this fact also allows us to date it with such certainty to the years just before his death. But the idea behind it took on immense importance in Palladio's development and his quest for a new type of aristocratic villa because it defines with great clarity all the elements essential to the running of a country estate, though here they are still clearly separated from the main residence.

Bibliography: Burns, 1979 (II), pp. 116-119; Lewis, 1981, pp. 102-104.

Design formerly believed to be of the Villa Poiana at Pojana Maggiore (London, R.I.B.A., XVI, 3).

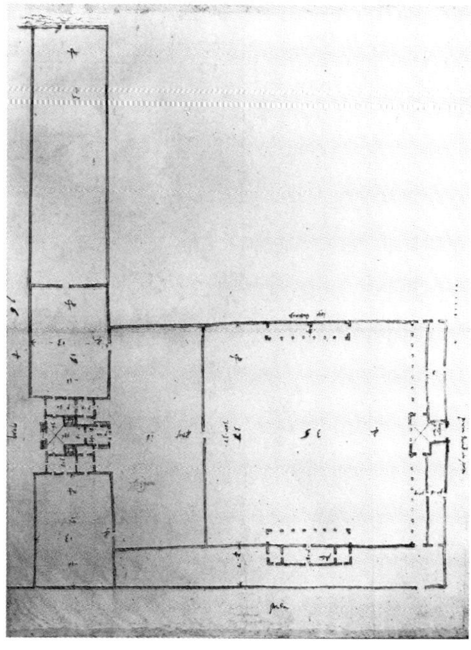

Villa Caldogno

46 Caldogno (Vicenza),
c. 1545; attribution not certain.

From Vicenza take the state highway no. 46 for Schio. At the turn-off for Thiene, after Motta, turn right to the centre of Caldogno. The villa stands near the church, with its left side on Via G. Zanella. It can be visited on Tuesday, 9-12 a.m., Thursday, 3-6 p.m., and Saturday, 9-12 a.m. For groups of over ten people it can also be visited at different times on other days by booking by phone (tel. 0444/585695).

This building in the centre of the town of Caldogno and containing one of the finest fresco cycles of the Cinquecento in the Veneto region has always been the object of dispute among Palladian scholars. It does not appear in the *Quattro Libri*—though this is also the case with other works attributed definitely to Palladio, especially early works—, there are mistakes in the execution, and the chronology is very uncertain: the date 1570 inscribed together with the name of Angelo di Losco Caldogno on the string-course of the façade corresponds closely to the time of the decoration inside, but not to the style of the building. So some scholars attribute the design to a master builder imitating the style of Palladio—for example, Pietro da Nanto—but the majority now tend to attribute the work to Palladio.
The villa has a very simple structure. Its rectangular bulk presents its side to the public road and is completely self-contained, so there can hardly have been any outbuildings for farmwork connected organically or stylistically to the manor house. In short, it seems to have been built mainly as a country house for leisure pursuits. The plan is based on a large rectangular chamber, illuminated by the windows of a fixed pattern set in the rear elevation and the elevation towards the loggia, which divides the three rooms on the right from the corresponding three on the left. Unfortunately the stairs serving the three floors of the building have been moved: in the nineteenth century they were reinserted in two turrets which, together with the terrace and flight of steps of the same period, have marred the original rear elevation.
The organization and proportions of the main façade are very close to what we find in the Villa Saraceno at Finale, dated to between 1545 and 1555, with scholars inclining towards the later 1540s. The central section, slightly projecting, is surmounted by a pediment and contains a loggia with three arches, with access provided by a flight of steps. But there are also evident affinities between the arches, framed with rusticated stonework and the elevation facing the river in the Villa Pisani at Bagnolo. At the same time the window mouldings, the arrangement of the plinth and the polygonal flight of steps seem to link it with the design of the Villa Poiana at Pojana Maggiore (see the drawing R.I.B.A., XVI, 4v).
In a final analysis, the handling of the elevation of the Villa Caldogno, with the intense chiaroscuro of the loggia set off against the smooth surface of the wall, is still suggestive of the example of Giulio Romano and seems to belong to Palladio's early period, in the later 1540s.
The lag between the conception of the design and the date 1570 mentioned above could be explained in various ways: by a delay (not uncommon) in construction, or the fact that the date could refer to the decoration. There is also the interesting theory that the villa may not have been commissioned by Angelo Caldogno but his relative Michele, who had a number of estates in the same area, as well as in Finale, close to the property of the Saraceno family with whom he was on terms of close friendship. Michele was a member of the circle of Palladio's acquaintances, and documents show he was frequently resident in a house of his at Caldogno down to the early 1560s, with an interval between 1545 and 1552 which might indicate the period when the new Palladian villa was being built. The villa then passed into the hands of Angelo di Losco Caldogno (who appears as its occupier from 1569 on): he may have been responsible for commissioning the decoration and putting his name on the front elevation together with the year it was completed. The frescoes are attributed mainly to Gianantonio Fasolo, with a subordinate part played by Giambattista Zelotti, and the scholars are unanimous in dating them to about 1570. They cover the simple, undecorated interiors, transforming them into a splendid architectural scenog-

Villa Caldogno, front and rear elevations.

raphy. Fasolo (of Vicenza) here attained the finest work of his career, fully expressing his naturalistic vein in the great *genre* scenes with depictions of the pleasures of life in the villa. The side walls of the loggia are decorated with a *Concert* and a *Banquet*, framed in imposing architectural compositions, while the vault is decorated with an *Olympus* thronged with gods arranged around the edges of an oval. The long salon has a fine beamed ceiling. The painter divided up the walls with a kind of portico and monochrome giants, remotely descended from Michelangelo, who support a frieze with *putti*and herms. Under the four arches so created on the longer sides there are two frescoes, a *Game of Cards* and an *Invitation to the Dance*, on the right-hand wall, and a *Concert* and a *Banquet* on the left-hand one. Over the doors there are female figures and contorted images of prisoners. The scenes are remarkable for the naturalistic energy of the figures, and at times one is tempted to see some of them as portraits of members of the Caldogno family. The colouring is soft and harmonious and a feeling of domestic peace hovers over everything.

The two large rooms on the left are attributed to Zelotti, now lacking energy for his work, and his workshop. Unfortunately they were extensively restored and repainted in the nineteenth century. The painter had recently completed his magnificent work at the Villa Emo at Fanzolo: here he divides the walls into panels, using large Corinthian columns, but fails to achieve a perfect equilibrium between decoration and representation. The frieze with *putti* and animals is too dominant in the south room, which depicts various episodes from the life of Scipio, while in the north room, with the *Stories of Sofonisba*, the figures acquire a marked vertical rhythm, with an almost Alexandrine elegance. The room also contains a brilliantly realistic portrait of Fasolo, in a *trompe l'oeil* doorway, together with a woman he is furtively embracing, surprised by an old woman who appears in the background. The middle room, decorated with scenes from the *Pastor Fido*, was begun by a collaborator of Zelotti on the left-hand side and completed in the seventeenth century by a Venetian painter, Giulio Carpioni. There are two highly interesting fireplaces in the largest rooms; they seem to belong to the circle of the Rubini. The left wing was not decorated; only in the early half of the eighteenth century was a frieze painted in the corner room facing north-east; it is attributed to Costantino Pasqualotto, also responsible for the small frescoes under the windows in the other rooms on the left and the monochrome figures in niches on the façade, unfortunately badly faded.

Bibliography: Muttoni, 1740, Index; Bertotti Scamozzi, 1778, pp. 52-53; Magrini, 1845, p. 286; Burger, 1909, p. 51; Pane, 1961, pp. 234-235; Crosato, 1962, pp. 99-103; Guiotto, 1964, pp. 73 ff.; Ackerman, 1967, pp. 41-43; Pallucchini, 1968, pp. 216-218; Zorzi, 1969, pp. 224-225; Cevese, 1971, I, pp. 134-138 and 1973, pp. 62-63; Puppi, 1973, pp. 259-261; Lewis, 1973 and 1981, pp. 152-154; Kubelik, 1974, p. 455; Burns, 1975, p. 190; Rigon, 1980, nos. 6-7; Canova, 1985, pp. 98-103; Muraro, 1986, pp. 272-277; Costant, 1987, pp. 67-68.

Plan of the Villa Thiene at Quinto Vicentino (Oxford, Worcester College).

Quinto Vicentino (Vicenza),
1545-1546; attribution certain, partially constructed and partially demolished and rebuilt.

Quinto Vicentino can be reached by the state highway from Vicenza, travelling towards Treviso. Immediately after Lisiera and the bridge over the River Tesina turn right and follow the embankment until the road takes a sharp bend to the left. Here stands the villa, the present town hall, in Via IV Novembre 4.

The history of the Villa Thiene at Quinto is a good example of the way Palladio's buildings diverge from the drawings published in the *Quattro Libri*. It was long considered, on the basis of the treatise, a total failure (due to lack of funds) to construct the colossal design printed in 1570, until the true autograph design turned up in a collection of papers which once belonged to Inigo Jones, the seventeenth century founder of English Palladianism. (The drawing is now at Worcester College, Oxford, H.T. 89; see Barbieri, 1971.) This, together with some maps from the early seventeenth century (published by Kubelik, 1974, pp. 453-454 and Puppi, 1974, p. 102) and the surveys carried out by Francesco Muttoni, showing what remained of the villa in the eighteenth century, means that the supposed failure is now seen in a new light. Besides, it is very difficult to relate Palladio's approach to construction—his concern with the nature of the site, including existing buildings, and his readiness to alter the design to meet different needs—to the abstract nature of the engraving in the treatise, totally foreign to any specific setting. It shows a complex structure, hard to decipher, comprising a sequence of courtyards and edifices presented symmetrically and frontally, with porticoes and atriums, all testifying to his absorbed

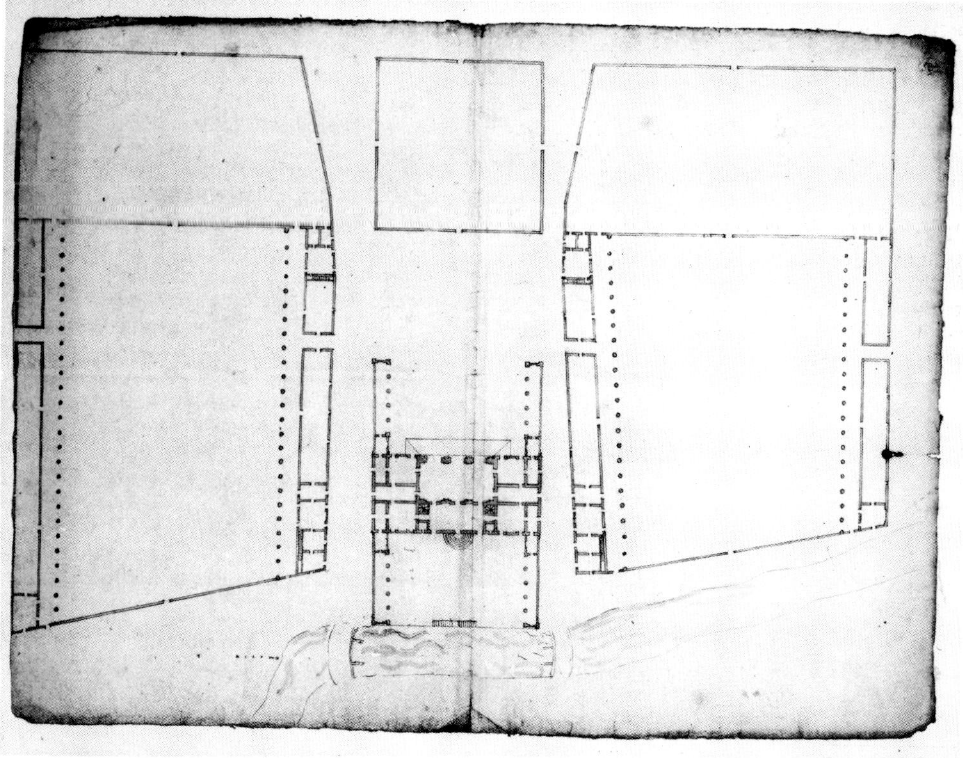

study of the baths and other edifices of imperial Rome. It has close affinities with the villa of the Ancients as represented by Vitruvius, likewise inserted in Palladio's treatise.

It is worth remembering that the Palazzo in *contrà* Santo Stefano in Vicenza, designed for his same patrons was also conceived as a revival of this particular archaeological model. This can be explained by the breadth of their culture (Palladio described them as "very learned in architecture"). In short, the illustration in the treatise referring to the villa must be seen as a later, imaginative reworking which is totally unrelated in fact to the morphology of the site, which was taken as an ineluctable quantity in the true design for the building.

In the design the main residential section is hemmed in on both sides by the two roads running parallel north and south of it. Beyond them there are two large courts with the outbuildings which, on the western side, follow the irregular course of the River Tesina and the road to Lisiera. The two elevations of the residence are closed off at each end by colonnades that frame two opposed courtyards and stretch westwards to the bank of the river. The plan, extremely wide but not deep, is divided into three sectors; at the centre is a large loggia with three arches leading into the chamber behind it, with two identical suites at the sides. Each of the suites can be seen as a self-contained complex; if seen from the sides, they look just like the traditional form of a Veneto house, with a long central chamber and other rooms at the sides. All this is quite remarkable if one thinks that the southern suite was really an old existing

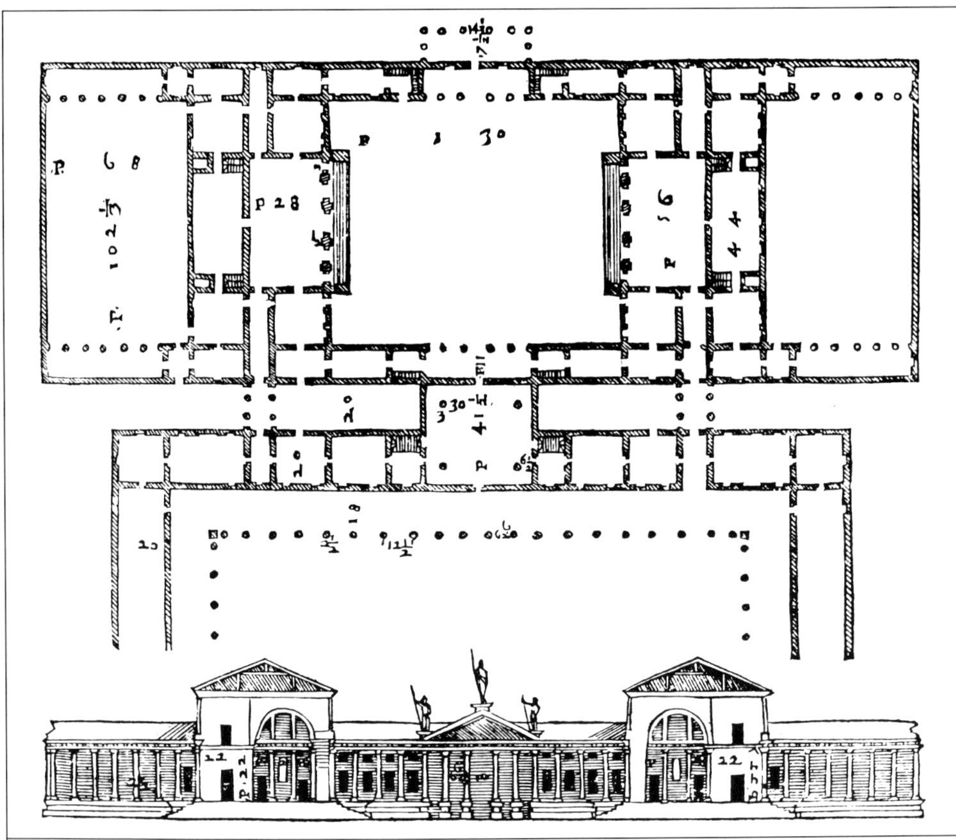

Drawing with the plan and elevation of the Villa Thiene at Quinto Vicentino (from the "Quattro Libri")

Villa Thiene (Quinto Vicentino), elevation onto the piazza and present elevation facing the countryside.

house set at a 90 degree angle to the new one, and that Palladio took it as his starting point to create a wholly original scheme.
The building was commissioned by the brothers Marcantonio and Adriano Thiene, by far the richest family in sixteenth century Vicenza, probably in the later 1540s, with 1546 as the most likely date, when the architect also resumed work on the design for an urban dwelling, after his second trip to Rome the year before. Construction then had to be broken off in 1560 because of the death of Marcantonio (his brother had died ten years earlier), when it had reached roughly the state in which Muttoni surveyed it in the early seventeenth century. His drawings show that about three-quarters of the main residence had been completed but the earlier building which formed the southern suite was still unchanged externally, and the porticoed wings were absent. In addition two early seventeenth century maps show that the line of outbuildings at the end of the courtyard had also been built. The part of the edifice completed had a line of giant Doric pilasters supporting the frieze. At the centre of the five intercolumns corresponding to the central section stood the three great arches of the loggia, flanked by rectangular windows surmounted by niches. The three intercolumns of the northern wing each contained a window and a smaller blind panel above them. The central section was also raised up an extra storey, and repeated the pilasters below together with three windows and side niches. There was no pediment, though the image of one was suggested by the gable of the roof. The structure was strongly reminiscent of Roman architecture, particularly Raphael's Villa Madama.
In the early years of the century the southern section—two-thirds of the whole building—was demolished, including the loggia, and replaced by the present structure, smaller in volume, which attempts to repeat the rhythm and composition of the original without much success. In short, all that is left of Palladio's building is the northern suite with the entrance from the road. What used to be the side of the villa is now the main elevation of the Quinto town hall, with its brickwork divided up by Doric pilasters, here coupled with niches in the centre, supporting a large pediment. Between the pilasters are set two rectangular windows and the entrance on the ground floor. The interior has been much tampered with, even recently, but it retains a small part of the frescoes mentioned by Palladio as the work of Giovanni De Mio, known as "l'Indemio," one of the most interesting Mannerist painters of Vicenza. His work covered the cloister vaulting of the large room to the left on the ground floor, decorated with monochrome festoons, masks and *putti*, which create a fantastic frame for five lively battle scenes from Greek and Roman mythology. The figures are set in contorted positions in sharp relief and the whole composition, of great beauty, is harmoniously united by the cool refined tones of colour. Other original Palladian rooms are the entrance hall and the other room on the left, parallel to the façade, which also contains remains of Cinquecento frescoes.

Bibliography: Vasari, 1568, p. 528; Palladio, 1570, l. II, p. 64; Muttoni, 1740, pp. 39-40; Bertotti Scamozzi, 1778, pp. 38-43; Burger, 1909, pp. 68-75; Magrini, 1845, pp. 238, 241; Pane, 1961, pp. 113-114; Crosato, 1962, p. 205; Forssman, 1965, p. 58; Ackerman, 1967, pp. 64-65; Zorzi, 1969, pp. 109-113; Cevese, 1971, II, pp. 538-539; Barbieri, 1971; Cevese, 1973, pp. 56-57; Puppi, 1973, pp. 261-265; Kubelik, 1974, pp. 453-454; Puppi, 1974, p. 102; Berger, 1977 and 1978, pp. 113-136; Lewis, 1981, pp. 92-96; Canova, 1985, pp. 104-107; Muraro, 1986, p. 186; Costant, 1987, pp. 55-56.

Villa Contarini

Piazzola sul Brenta (Padua),
1546; attribution not certain, later extended and remodelled.

Leaving from Vicenza, take the road for Padua, then turn off at Torri di Quartesolo and go to Camisano. From Camisano the road goes on to Piazzola sul Brenta. The sumptuous villa is in the middle of the town, facing a monumental colonnaded piazza across the canal.

An insistent seventeenth century tradition led scholars to study the Villa Contarini Camerini in quest of some clue to Palladio's presence at Piazzola, where the Contarini family was said to have summoned him to design their villa. Various facts concur in supporting the claim. Of course no one would dare to credit him with the present imposing, theatrical baroque plan of the building, which belongs to the later seventeenth century. But if one were to imagine the central nucleus of the complex stripped of its overcharged decoration and with the relation between the lateral turrets and the central block corrected (by making the latter one storey lower), the result would exactly resemble the depiction of the Cinquecento Villa Contarini (published in Puppi, 1975). It stood on the same site as now, flanked by two straight wings of porticoed outbuildings and fronted by a large rectangular court. This villa makes the suggested link with Palladio quite credible. Note, for example, how the design of the elevation, framed by lateral towers, is very close to the arrangement of the Villa Pisani at Bagnolo, while the repeated use of the *serliana* (at the base of the turrets and on the *piano nobile*) is one of the hallmarks of Palladio's work in the 1540s, a feature he borrowed from Sebastiano Serlio.

Villa Contarini, central elevation (seventeenth century addition).

In addition, the history of the buildings reveals that Andrea did receive a commission for work at Piazzola from Paolo Contarini, a member of one of the most powerful Venetian families and related to the Giacomo Contarini of the San Samuele branch of the family, in whose house in Venice Palladio stayed for a long period. The original conception and the laying of the foundations can be dated to about 1546, the date carved on the base of the building at the side of the present staircase. Construction work was then held up considerably, but a decade later, in 1556, work was going ahead on the mouldings of the doors and windows. From this period there is an interesting legal document requiring the workmen supplying the stones (from quarries in the Berici mountains) to speed up. The document enables us to identify the person who in all probability acted as intermediary between Contarini and Palladio, in view of the excellent relationship he enjoyed with both men. The marble was taken from Vicenza to Piazzola by water and while awaiting the barges it was stored in a house overlooking the port of Isola (now Piazza Matteotti) belonging to Antenore Pagello, who appears in the *Quattro Libri* as "highly learned" in architecture. Moreover Palladio is also connected with the Cinquecento Villa Contarini by the fact that work at Piazzola was supervised by the mason Girolamo Rubini, his collaborator in the construction of the Villa Pisani at Montagnana in 1553. Considering the care with which Palladio chose his workmen, re-employing the same ones on many different projects, it is hardly likely to have been a mere coincidence.

We still have to find out exactly how the Cinquecento design of the main residence (completed and inhabited only in 1565), with its outbuildings at the sides and spacious forecourt, came to be retained as the starting point of the magniloquent seventeenth century baroque extensions, instead of being demolished.

Bibliography: Camerini, 1925; Zorzi, 1969, pp. 62-66; Puppi, 1973, p. 265; 1974, pp. 103-104 and 1975; Semenzato, 1973, pp. 21-25; Battilotti, 1977, p. 232.

Villa Arnaldi

Meledo Alto di Sarego (Vicenza), 1547 and 1565; attribution certain, partially completed and then remodelled.

From Vicenza take the state highway for Verona as far as Alte Ceccato. Here turn left towards Lonigo and after a few kilometres you come to Meledo Basso. A road on the left, skirting the old church, climbs up the hillside to Meledo Alto. The former Villa Arnaldi stands half-way up the slope. A recent rectangular gateway provides access to the courtyard and to the left the old chapel can just be identified by its shed roof and central oculus.

In about 1547 Vincenzo Arnaldi, a nobleman of Vicenza, decided to restructure an old villa complex on the hillside of Meledo, which still exists though much damaged and almost unrecognizable. The pages of an account book dated to the above year show that he intended to rebuild the loggia of the main residence and paint it with imitation marble or landscapes, enlarge the courtyard on the lower side and join the little oratory of San Nicolò to the house to form a continuous façade, including the front entrance, facing the road. The documents also comprise three sketches of the plan and a rough indication of the elevation which are accepted as autograph drawings by Palladio. They outline the new layout of the whole complex as three sides of a rectangular court. The shorter side facing west, with the main entrance, has a rustic portico mirrored by an identical one on the opposite side; while the family residence (which is fairly shallow and dilated lengthwise) takes up the whole of the north side, bordering on the road at the back. The chapel occupies the north-west corner with its façade facing west.
So Palladio's first plan united all the existing structures, which certainly included the oratory and the family residence as well as a Gothic outhouse that still exists (remodelled in later periods) to the right of the entrance. In this way he gave the complex a regular perimeter and obtained two symmetrical outbuildings attached to the sides of the main residence. His first idea for the latter was a loggia with four columns and five intercolumns, but he then fell back on a scheme that looks more economical, as it makes fuller use of the existing structure: a narrower loggia, two storeys high (not three), and three simple arches borne on pillars with two trabeated windows with oculi above.
In 1550 work was definitely under way and the loggia was being built. So it appears that Palladio's scheme was executed, at least in part. Besides, the three arches with the rectangular windows at the sides are still to be seen, though bricked up and without the oculi, in the decayed building that now exists, where they are surmounted by three widely spaced windows, also dating from the sixteenth century. But work must have been broken off for some time, for it was only in 1565 that Arnaldi commissioned Palladio to produce a design for the ceilings of the two rooms behind the loggia. The drawing was promptly forwarded from Venice on 23 February, together with explanations for the masons and a promise to check the work soon after. As far as we can tell from the drawing, which has come down to us with the letter and presupposes a planimetric survey, Palladio intended identical vaulted ceilings for both rooms, with two lunettes in each corner and a large panel in the centre, evidently meant to contain a fresco.
This work was never carried out, and the two rooms still have the beamed ceilings. But two fine fireplaces have survived, together with two fragments of frescoes in the panel over the door, and on the floor above a very fine ceiling with painted beams, all sixteenth century work. And it is also clear that the alterations to the two outhouses planned in 1547 were never carried out. As late as 1575, on the eve of Arnaldi's death, building materials were piled up in the house and courtyard. A map from the end of the century (published in Puppi, 1974, pp. 96-97) seems to show the situation described by the nobleman in his will, drawn up in 1566; it depicts the court with the residence and its loggia, the chapel, well and fifteenth century outhouse. A wall may have been built to unite the façade of the church (now converted into a home) and the old outbuilding, which until a few years ago still had a fine early Cinquecento door in the middle, with a triangular tympanum and heraldic bearings on the architrave. The fine outhouse on the east side dates from the sec-

ond half of the eighteenth century and is work of Enea Arnaldi of Vicenza, who was also the owner of the property. The villa's history is rich in interest, quite beyond the modesty of the present complex, for it reveals an approach not at all uncommon in Palladio's work, based on respect for existing structures and the ability to create a new image with just a few limited alterations. It should also be noticed that the outbuildings gradually acquire far greater importance in the design of the villa complex.

Bibliography: Magrini, 1845, pp. 74-75; Zorzi, 1969, pp. 227-228; Cevese, 1971, II, pp. 585-586; Puppi, 1973, pp. 371-372 and 1974, pp. 96-97; Burns, 1975, pp. 221-222 and 1979, pp. 15-16; Lewis, 1981, pp. 118-120.

Villa Saraceno

Finale di Agugliaro (Vicenza),
c. 1548; attribution certain.

From Vicenza take the state highway no. 247 for Noventa Vicentina. Go past the turn-off for Agugliaro on the left and 2 km later take the next road on the left (Via Finale) which stretches away into the countryside flanked by a row of poplars. The villa stands about 300 metres down the road on the left-hand side

The villa was built in the fifth or sixth decade of the sixteenth century by Biagio Saraceno of Vicenza. It is definitely by Palladio, who published the plan and elevation in the *Quattro Libri*. But it is not to be expected that the long ranges of porticoes, shown in the treatise as stretching out from the manor to form a large rectangular court with circular turrets at the two corners, were ever actually constructed at Finale. All that was built was the central block, now flanked on one side by a segment of portico.
The villa is in a disturbingly derelict state; but the simple restraint of this building, with its limited architectural vocabulary, remains striking. The whole design turns on the slight projection of the central section of the façade to contain the loggia with its three arches resting directly on pillars (as at the Villa Godi), with a flight of steps leading up to it and crowned with a pediment. Yet it is wonderfully harmonious in the carefully gauged relationship between the elements and the interplay between the brightness of the surfaces, the shadow of the arches and the chiaroscuro of the beautiful cornice.
The dating of the villa formerly divided scholars into two groups, one maintaining it was an early design and the other placing it at about 1560. Recently discovered documents narrowed the date down to the period falling between two appraisals of the property's value, dated respectively 1546 and 1555. The first refers to the old manor house; the second mentions the "casa nova nondum finita." The words "not yet finished" seem to suggest a date close to 1555, except for the bareness of the architectural vocabulary which relates the Villa Saraceno to Palladio's other early works (the Villa Godi at Lonedo, Muzani at Malo or Gazzotti at Bertesina) and would make more sense if the design went back to the 1540s. The self-enclosed block-like structure, indifferent to the setting, and the handling of the façade also relate closely to the Villa Caldogno at Caldogno and Zeno at Cessalto. But the chronology of these buildings is also very uncertain and cannot be accurately placed in the line of Palladio's development.
As for the service structures depicted in the *Quattro Libri*, it is certain work never began on them in Palladio's lifetime, so that some scholars doubt whether they were ever really part of the original plan, especially since the enclosed character of the villa seems complete in itself, like the villa at Caldogno, which also lacks outbuildings. Consequently they may have been added to the design when the plates were being prepared for printing in 1570. Actually two outhouses were built at the beginning of the seventeenth century, while towards the end of the same century the one to the east was replaced by a second colonnade, described as "noble," later destroyed by fire in 1798. The present outhouse is simply a reconstruction of it built at the start of the last century. In this sequence of events it is important to note how an attempt was made to complete the villa to fit the design published in the treatise—the same thing happened at the Palazzo Chiericati in Vicenza and the Villa Trissino at Meledo.
The villa of the Saraceno family (inherited by the Caldognos at the beginning of the seventeenth century) was altered in numerous other ways over the years; at first the changes marred the original design then they restored it. The interior was remodelled at various times to meet the changing needs of the owners, so that the layout and proportions of Palladio's rooms have been lost. In the later seventeenth century numerous windows and doors were added, then closed up again in the nineteenth century when the Peruzzi family, the new owners, restored the façade to its original state, though the outline of the alterations can still be glimpsed under the plasterwork. There have also been alterations to the staircase, which had only a single archway in the seventeenth century but has been rather coarsely restored to its original width in this century.
Of the decoration commissioned by Saraceno all that remains are the tattered frescoes of

Drawing with plan and elevation of the Villa Saraceno (from the "Quattro Libri").

Villa Saraceno, front elevation.

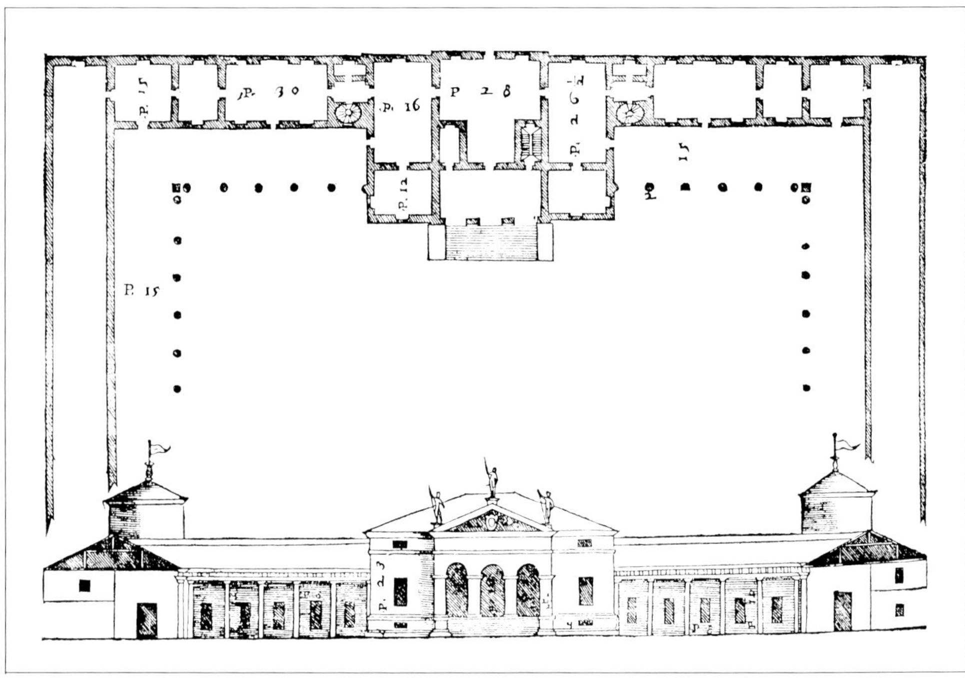

Villa Saraceno, vault of the loggia with frescoes.

the loggia, salon and west room. The ceiling of the loggia bears the signs of an octagon with a representation of Riches, surrounded by monochrome figures, paintings and medallions with scenes from Roman history. Above the central doorway there is a clumsy portrait of a warrior, traditionally identified with Biagio Saraceno, the builder of the house. All these paintings are by a very modest artist. The frieze in the west room is of higher quality (some scholars attribute it to Brusasorci): it is clearly a work of the Roman school and much damaged, as is that in the central chamber depicting *putti* against volutes and panels with landscapes. The wooden ceiling with painted beams is exceptionally beautiful.

Bibliography: Vasari, 1568, p. 528; Palladio, 1570, l. II, p. 56; Muttoni, 1740, p. 29; Bertotti Scamozzi, 1778, p. 36; Magrini, 1845, pp. 75, 241; Burger, 1909, pp. 49-52; Pane, 1961, pp. 227-228; Crosato, 1962, pp. 117-118; Ackerman, 1967, pp. 46-47; Zorzi, 1969, pp. 72-74; Cevese, 1971, I, pp. 124-125 and 1973, pp. 63-64; Puppi, 1973, pp. 258-259; Kubelik, 1979, pp. 180-181; Rigon, 1980, no. 5; Muraro, 1981-1982 and 1986, p. 268; Canova, 1985, pp. 94-97; Bödefeld-Hinz, 1987, pp. 111-112; Costant, 1987, p. 51; Carunchio-Cavaggioni-Del Zoppo, 1987.

Villa Angarano

60 Angarano di Bassano del Grappa (Vicenza),
1548; attribution certain, only the outbuildings remain.

Coming from Vicenza-Marostica, one comes to Angarano just before Bassano's town centre, on the near side of the Brenta river, towards Campese. The villa (now known as the Villa Bianchi-Michiel) stands not far from the suburb.

One of the people closest to Palladio, helping to build his career, protecting him affectionately and in some cases even assisting him financially was Giacomo Angarano, a nobleman of Vicenza. Andrea expressed his gratitude by dedicating the first two books of his treatise on architecture to him. The second volume also contains two buildings he designed for his friend; one a city mansion which was begun but never completed, and the other a villa which Palladio states was built at Angarano, near Bassano.
This building can be identified with the present Villa Bianchi Michiel, to the south of the town, but all that we have now are two outhouses. (A family chapel was inserted in the right-hand one in the early eighteenth century.) Just as shown in the engraving in the *Quattro Libri*, the outhouses, with their sober Doric colonnade, are arranged in two symmetrical wings enclosing the rectangular courtyard, and some scholars hold that these are the only art or the complex ever completed. When Vincenzo Gadenigo, in the late seventeenth or early eighteenth century, commissioned an unknown but clearly very able architect to build the present manor house, there was no trace of the Palladian building. A seventeenth century map (published by Zorzi, 1969, figs. 116-117) shows only a modest farm house with a well in front of it. So whether Palladio's design was never built or was demolished for whatever reason before the map was drawn remains a mystery. What is certain is that in 1548 work at Angarano was going ahead fast and Palladio was often present, so the design tends to be dated to those years.
In the absence of any concrete information we have to fall back on the drawings in the *Quattro Libri*, though as we have seen this is not a faithful guide to the original design. Still, it is interesting to see how the middle section of the elevation of the residential nucleus with its *serliana* (flanked by giant columns supporting a pediment) repeats the same motif that we found at the slightly earlier Villa Contarini at Piazzola, as well as other early works. But what stands out most powerfully and distinguishes Villa Angarano from previous designs is the fact that here Palladio has achieved a breakthrough in the creation of the country house, functionally and figuratively suited to the new needs of the aristocracy, which were intended to project an ideal image of themselves and at the same time help them to administer their country estates. After the important but partial experiments at the Villa Thiene at Quinto or the designs for Pagliarino, Palladio came to design a complex in which the outbuildings are not detached from the main residence but fused with it and subordinated, naturally, to the central block, which is set slightly forward and "ennobled" by the sacred element of the pediment yet united with the rest through their common classical vocabulary.

Bibliography: Vasari, 1568, p. 528; Palladio, 1570, 1.II, p. 63; Muttoni, 1740, p. 37; Bertotti Scamozzi, 1781, p. 31; Temanza, 1778, p. 361; Magrini, 1845, pp. 78, 238, 240; Burger, 1909, p. 26-30; Pane, 1961, pp. 112, nos. 37, 113; Ackerman, 1967, p. 64; Zorzi, 1969, pp. 77-82; Cevese, 1971, II, p. 325; Puppi, 1973, pp. 271-273; Lewis, 1973, pp. 272-273 and 1981, pp. 157-158; Canova, 1985, pp. 120-123; Costant, 1987, p. 64.

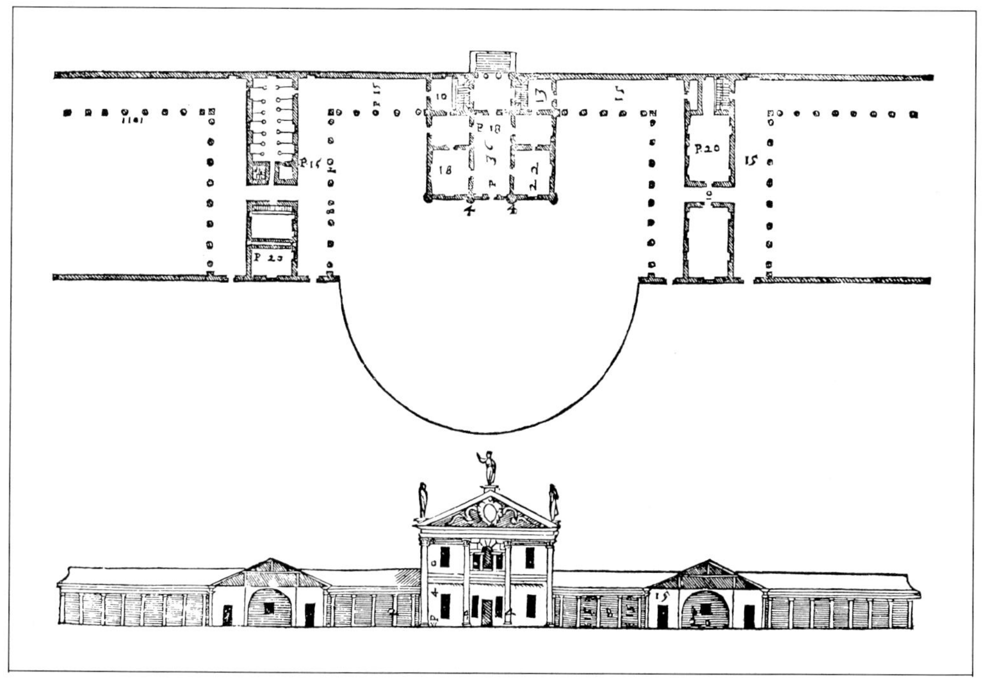

Drawing of the plan and elevation of the Villa Angarano (from the "Quattro Libri").

Villa Angarano, view of the whole complex, with the outbuildings by Palladio.

Villa Poiana

Drawing of the plan and elevation of the Villa Poiana (from the "Quattro Libri").

62 Pojana Maggiore (Vicenza), c. 1550; attribution certain.

From Vicenza follow the Riviera Berica (state highway no. 247) as far as Noventa Vicentina, then continue to Pojana Maggiore. The villa is on the far edge of the town, to the left, on the road to Montagnana. It can be visited every day between 3 p.m. and 4 p.m. At other times, for groups of visitors, by telephone booking (tel. 0444/898554).

Definitely one of Palladio's finest villas, this is a model of purity in its proportions, originality of composition and structural simplicity. The edifice rests on a low plinth, and the middle section of the elevation, comprising the atrium, is set almost imperceptibly forward from it. At the centre of the atrium is a *serliana* (or Venetian window). This is flanked by two windows and receded by a flight of steps, while its sharp-edged cornice is set directly in the wall; it is surmounted by a double arched lintel containing five *tondi*. The pediment, thanks to its split base, does not disturb the form of the arch below the *serliana* and allows light to flood the smooth wall surface, highlighting the chiaroscuro of the apertures in the atrium. The same pattern is repeated in a flatter version on the rear elevation where, however, it is broken up by the more numerous apertures which let light into the salon. The interior is unexpectedly monumental, the effect being achieved by the perfect proportions; it is organized symmetrically around the sides of the central axis formed by the atrium, roofed with a transept in the centre and with a long, narrow barrel-vaulted salon. As is often the case in Palladio's works, the interplay of the vaulting in the semi-basement rooms is extremely effective. The record provided by the *Quattro Libri* makes the attribution to Palladio certain. The villa was commissioned by Bonifacio Poiana, a *cavaliere* of Vicenza, whose family vaunted their ancient military prowess, staunchly faithful to the Venetian Republic, and possessed an almost feudal power over the territories bearing their name. The villa was demonstrably unfinished in 1555, so that scholars tend almost unanimously to date the design to a few years before this date, in about 1550. By 1563 construction was complete, together with the decoration of the interior, which Palladio himself declares to be the work of the painters Bernardino India and Anselmo Canera and the sculptor Bartolomeo Ridolfi, all of Verona. Not all the critics agree on how to allot the paintings to the various hands, and there is even the suggestion that a third painter was also at work. Anselmo Canera is generally credited with the paintings in the atrium and central hall. Fake stucco cornices and delicate flower patterns divide up the transept of the atrium into pan-

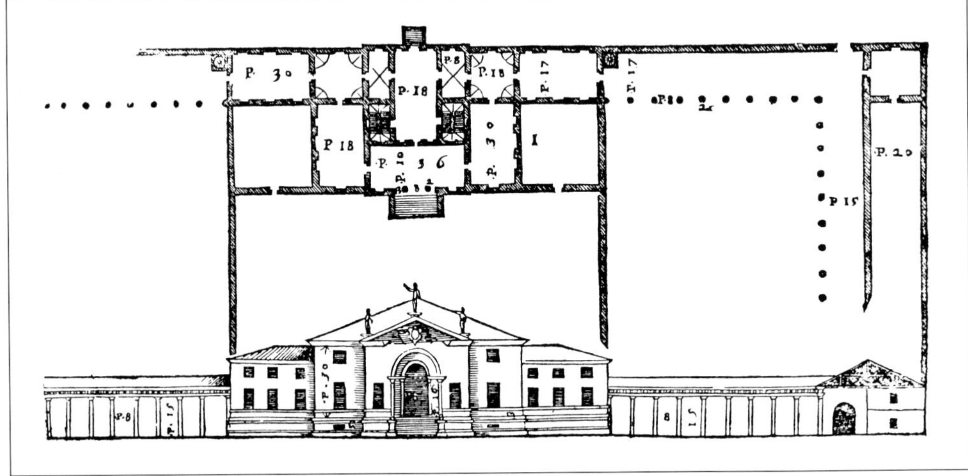

Villa Poiana, front elevation and Chamber of the Emperors with frescoes attributed to Bernardino India.

els containing monochrome depictions of river gods and medallions, with an octagon in the centre representing Fortune.
The inside wall over the doorway depicts the bust of Bonifacio Poiana by Bartolomeo Ridolfi, with above it military trophies and the family coat of arms. The two lunettes at the sides contain allegorical scenes; they are attributed conjecturally to an artist in the circle of Giambattista Zelotti. The other three medallions in the vault of the salon also display the influence of Veronese on Canera and his qualities as a colourist: they depict Olympus (in the centre), Mercury, and Spring, Baccus and Ceres (at the sides).
The hand of Bernardino India is evident in the two rooms to the right. In the larger, the female figures (reminiscent of Parmigianino) and the muscular male nudes of the divinities of Olympus fill the centre of the pavilion ceiling, divided up by delicate stucco-framed panels by Ridolfi containing the Triumphs of the Roman emperors. *Trompe l'oeil* Ionic columns frame the walls, surrounding bronze-coloured statues of emperors and landscapes, while an archway spans a group of figures (the Poiana family, perhaps?) in classical garments, kneeling before the statue of Peace—a clear allusion to the peace enjoyed by the mainland nobility after the dark years of the War of the League of Cambrai, which now allows them to taste the pleasures of life in the villa. The small adjacent chamber (generally attributed to Bernardino India, though some experts see it as the work of Eliodoro Forbicini) is completely covered with delightful grotesques, save for the lunettes which contain landscapes with ruins. The statues of Jove and Neptune, set at the sides of the main staircase, were executed in 1648 by Girolamo Albanese.
The outbuildings of Villa Poiana were never completed (the one on the left is eighteenth century work). They appear in the illustration in the *Quattro Libri* and are confirmed by an autograph drawing by Palladio which shows one of the phases in the development of the design (London, R.I.B.A., XVI, 4). The residential nucleus was meant to be flanked by two short, rather lower, wings, communicating with the porticoes and continued at right angles to form two sides each of the large flanking courtyards.
Compared with the arrangement at the Villa Angarano, Villa Poiana represents an intermediate phase in which the outhouses are visually separate from the residence, as at the Villa Thiene at Quinto or even more clearly in the design for Villa Pagliarino. The similarities with the latter are remarkable; so much so that it seems to be a faithful repetition of it. As for the residence, the plans on the *recto* and *verso* of the drawing mentioned before are close to the built form of Villa Poiana but they are turned at an angle of 180 degrees compared to it, and show the *serliana* in the façade without the oculi, while the central arch is borne on columns instead of pillars. In fact the pattern of the *serliana* constructed is unique in Palladio's work and he seems, in the treatise, to have felt the need to omit a *serliana* whenever the two rectangular apertures are absent together with the oculi, so that only the central arch is left. The design clearly stems from Bramante, and seems to be derived from the nymphaeum of Gennazzano near Rome, or else from certain drawings by Giuliano Sangallo the Younger. But at the same time it is the outcome of a lengthy course of experimenting with the patterns of the *serliana*, which led to the design of the loggias of the Basilica in Vicenza; an earlier version is quite close to the design found at the Villa Poiana, and is to be found in the façade of the Villa Valmarana at Vigardolo. Villa Poiana was carefully restored at the end of the 1960s by the *Ente per le Ville Venete*, its present owner. During the work, a window that disfigured the pediment of the façade was closed up and the original semicircular staircase of the rear elevation was found and restored. But unfortunately the failure to find any use for this favoured building means that it is now beginning to decay again.

Bibliography: Vasari, 1568, p. 528; Palladio, 1570, 1.II, p. 58; Muttoni, 1740, p. 31; Bertotti Scamozzi, 1778, pp. 33-35; Magrini, 1845, pp. LXXII, 240; Burger, 1909, pp. 98-102; Pane, 1961, pp. 226 ff.; Crosato, 1962, pp. 170-172; Dalla Pozza, 1965, p. 56; Forssman, 1965, p. 190 ff.; Ackerman, 1967, pp. 62-64; Cevese, 1968 (II); Wilinski, 1968; Zorzi, 1969, pp. 83-87; Cevese, 1971, I, pp. 112-121 and 1973, pp. 64-65; Puppi, 1973, pp. 274-277; Rigon, 1980, no. 8; Muraro, 1981-1982 and 1986, p. 188; Canova, 1985, pp. 108-119, Bödefeld-Hinz, 1987, pp. 129- 131; Costant, 1987, pp. 69-70.

Villa Zeno

Donegal di Cessalto (Treviso), c. 1550 (?); attribution certain.

Cessalto is easily reached from the exit on the A4 motorway of the same name, in the stretch between Mestre and Venice. The villa is in the locality called Donegal, between Cessalto and Céggia, on the road flanking the Piavon canal.

Were it not for Palladio's own testimony in the *Quattro Libri*, proving the design to be his, this villa might well have never been noticed by the scholars. Apart from the highly suspect mistakes in execution and what are obviously subsequent tamperings with the building, it poses the problem of why the elevations have been swapped round: the façade facing the road is unpretentious, indeed it has been practically featureless ever since the thermal window in the centre of the upper storey was unfortunately closed up and replaced by four close-set rectangular windows that repeat the rhythm of those lower down (perhaps originally arched), at the sides of a simple trabeated door. The surface is plain, only marked by horizontal string courses (not in the original plan) that join up the windows sills and architraves, while the central section is not set forward, so that the small pediment above it strikes one as almost out of place.
To the sides of this elevation—according to the treatise—there were to have been two porticoed wings of outhouses which then turned at right angles to reach the road. They were most probably never built and certainly there is no trace of them: the structures at the side of the building now are of a later date.
The rear elevation is quite different. It projects slightly in the centre, and this part is surmounted by a pediment and screened by three slender arches resting on pillars, providing access to the portico. Logically this ought to be the main elevation, as at the Villa Saraceno at Finale or the Villa Caldogno at Caldogno, to mention only two buildings with the same kind of three-arched portico; while the other façade with its obviously functional design is similar to that of the Villa Foscari at Malcontenta, which looks out onto the countryside. The ground plan—as shown in the

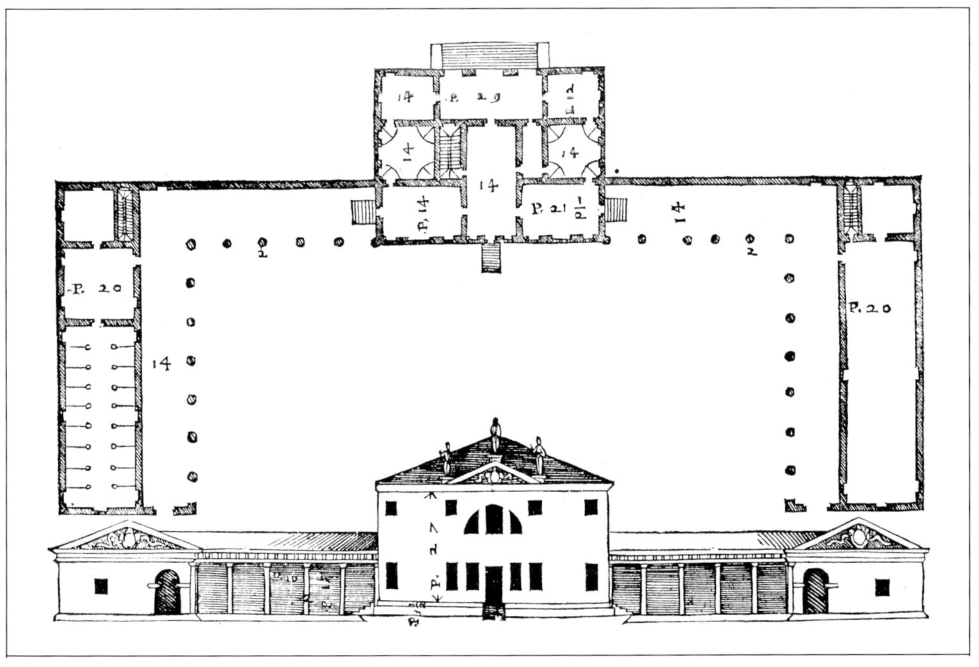

Drawing with the plan and elevation of the Villa Zeno (from the "Quattro Libri").

Villa Zeno, view of the front.

Quattro Libri, because the building's interior has been extensively remodelled—is also affected by the reversal, so that from the roadway access is provided by a very poor staircase directly into the main salon, without the kind of screen normally provided by a portico or hallway.

Moreover, in the treatise the illustration also shows the villa from the same side, linking it to the image of the Villa Pisani at Bagnolo, whose design is closely related to this one. This seems to suggest that the explanation lies in Palladio's desire to provide a homogeneous image of all his villas, with the porticoes facing the reader. But we know that at Bagnolo the main façade was the one with the three arches facing the river, the main line of communication; while at Cessalto both the road and the Piavon canal pass to the south, in front of the courtyard of the villa. It would be interesting to find out if the position of the road and waterway in the sixteenth century were the same as now, or if there used to be some form of access on the same side as the portico.

There are also difficulties in fixing the villa's date, history, and relation to earlier buildings on the site, as we have no document that sheds any light on it. We only know it was built before 1566, when a statement was made to the Venetian fiscal authorities, showing it was part of an estate comprising 450 fields. The same year Vasari knew of it through Palladio and mentioned it in his *Lives* in 1568. Some scholars put it at about 1565, others at about 1558-1559, when the client, Marco Zeno, a Venetian patrician, was *podestà* in Vicenza and so could have met the architect, though an earlier acquaintance can hardly be ruled out. The building offers evident analogies in its plan and elevations with other Palladian villas of the early period, like the Villa Pisani at Bagnolo, Villa Saraceno at Finale and Villa Caldogno at Caldogno, as well as the Villa Poiana at Pojana and that designed for Bartolomeo Pagliarino, all previous to 1550.

Bibliography: Vasari, 1568, p. 530; Palladio, 1570, 1. II, p. 49; Muttoni, 1740, pp. 22 ff.; Bertotti Scamozzi, 1781, pp. 33-34; Magrini, 1845, p. 240; Burger, 1909, pp. 47-49; Pane, 1961, pp. 225-227; Wittkower, 1964, pp. 216-218; Ackerman, 1967, p. 43; Zorzi, 1969, pp. 184-186; Cevese, 1973, p. 77; Lewis, 1973, pp. 371-372; Puppi, 1973, pp. 373-375; Fairbairn, in Burns, 1975, pp. 190-191; Canova, 1985, pp. 220-223; Muraro, 1986, p. 256; Costant, pp. 97-98.

Villa Schio

Façade of the Villa Schio (by Ottavio Bertotti-Scamozzi, in Le fabbriche e i disegni di Andrea Palladio, vol. II, Vicenza 1778).

Montecchio Precalcino (Vicenza), 1552; attribution not certain, demolished.

The villa was situated in the hamlet of Preara, to the north of Montecchio Precalcino, reached from Vicenza by taking the road for Bassano and turning left at the bridge at Passo di Riva.

This villa no longer exists and all we have is a survey of it conducted by Ottavio Bertotti Scamozzi in the late eighteenth century. On the basis of a persistent tradition Scamozzi included it in Palladio's works though he pointed out that it was not an outstanding building, being the adaptation of an earlier structure.
A reliable critical appraisal is obviously out of the question. Documents show it as close in type to the Villa Forni, no great distance away from it, but enclosed within two turrets. All the same the attribution to Palladio is justified by various circumstances. The villa belonged to Bernardo Schio, whom Palladio mentions as a gentlemen of Vicenza with an interest in architecture, while an inventory of 1566 shows that Palladio supplied him with the drawings for the façade of the *palazzetto* in Borgo Pusterla in Vicenza. (This must have been before 1561, when we know work and already begun on the new façade.) The inventory also tells us that the contract for work on the villa was drawn up at the end of 1552 between Sebastiano Schio (Bernardo's father) and the master builder Pietro da Nanto (to whom some scholars also attribute the design); we also learn that the expenses ledger was closed in 1560, marking the completion of work.
So there is no reason to exclude the possibility that Palladio produced the designs for the villa. Schio might well have been prompted to restructure his country house by the desire to emulate the nearby Villa Forni. An interesting conjecture suggests this was designed by Palladio at the start of the 1540s for the Brandizio family, whose property bordered on the Schio estates, while there was a cordial friendship between the two families.

Bibliography: Bertotti Scamozzi, 1778, pp. 45-47; Magrini, 1845, p. 280; Pane, 1961, p. 105; Zorzi, 1969, pp. 223-224; Puppi, 1973, p. 228; Zaupa, 1989.

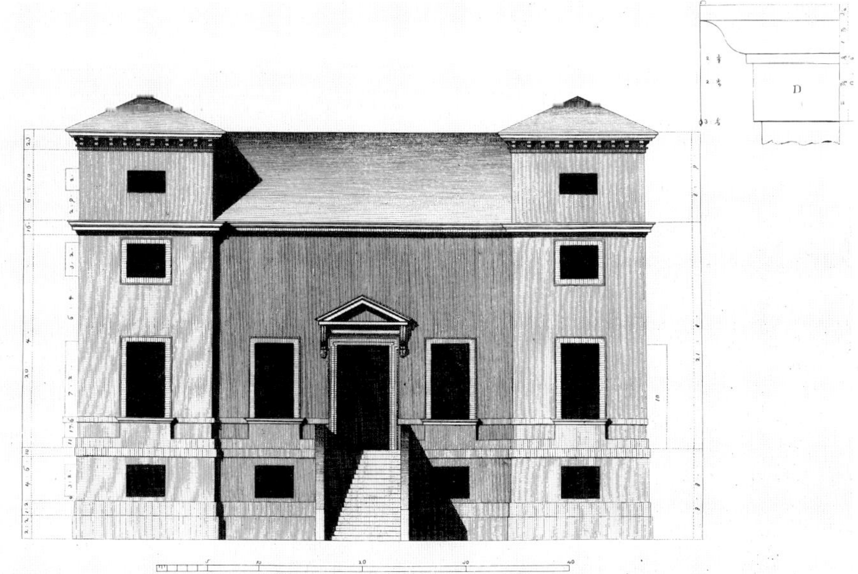

Villa Pisani

68 Montagnana (Padua),
1552; attribution certain.

To reach Montagnana from Vicenza take the state highway no. 247 as far as Noventa Vicentina, then continue as far as Pojana Maggiore. The villa stands at the junction between the road skirting the medieval town walls and the one leading out of the town towards Padua. It can be visited by prior telephone request to the owner, *signora* Francesca Placco (tel. 0429/81368).

The villa stands at a crossroads just outside the walls of Montagnana. The front elevation looks onto the road leading out of the town towards Padua and the side faces the road flanking the old town walls and moat. It can be described as a hybrid between the villas in the open countryside and the urban *palazzo*, the first of a new series of suburban villas by Palladio; their immediate predecessor is the Palazzo Chiericati in Vicenza—regarded by some as a kind of "seaside villa" because of its open structure and the way it used to face the esplanade and port on the Bacchiglione, known as the "Isola." It is also close to subsequent designs such as the Villa Cornaro at Piombino Dese and the Palazzo Antonini in Udine.

The twofold character of the Villa Pisani is evident in the differences between the two main elevations. The two-storey building seen from the roadway looks like a severe, self-enclosed block, almost neoclassical in its elegance and rigidity. The side, flanked on the right by a little seventeenth century family chapel, is only enlivened in the middle by

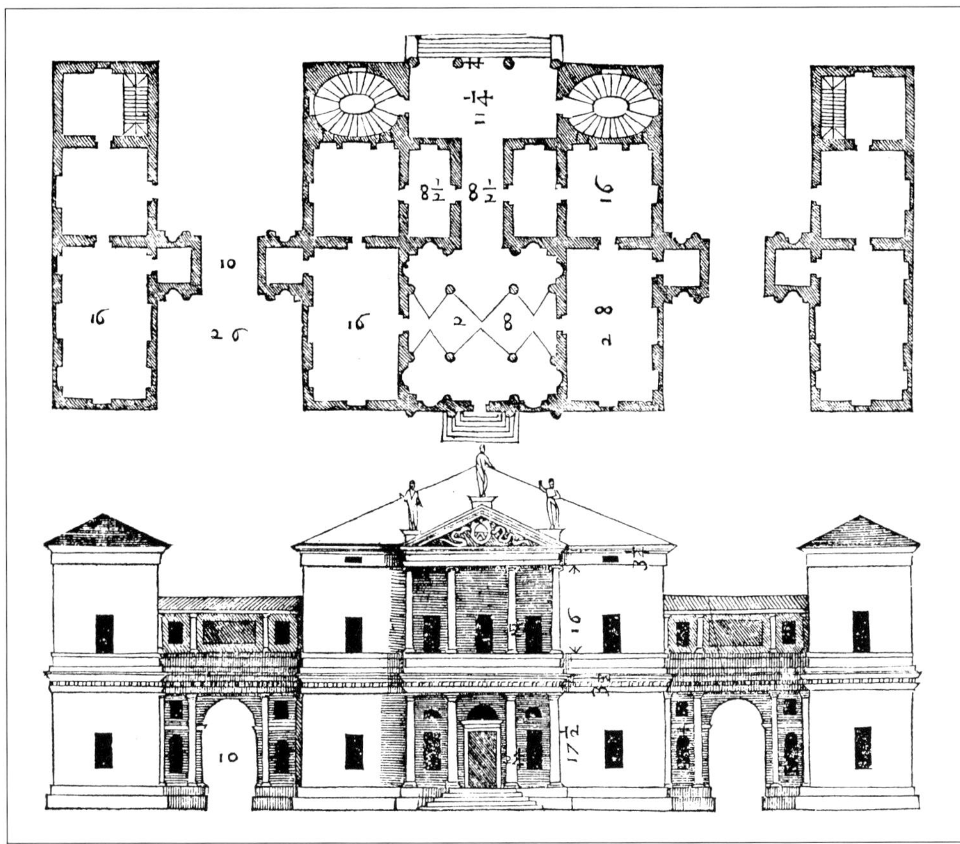

Drawing of the plan and elevation of the Villa Pisani at Montagnana (from the "Quattro Libri").

Villa Pisani (Montagnana), views of the whole complex with the elevation onto the road and the elevation onto the garden.

the slightly projecting double order of Doric and Ionic semi-columns (respectively on the lower and upper storeys) supporting the pediment with the arms of the Pisani family flanked by two winged figures of Fame, the work of Alessandro Vittoria. The fine Doric frieze dividing the two storeys runs all round the building; the windows are "sharp-edged," without a cornice, which is reserved for the slender main doorway. The elevation facing onto the garden, though it repeats the same scheme as the elevation onto the road, is enlivened by setting the middle section slightly forward; it stands open with a double loggia that provides a screen between exterior and interior and creates a pleasant half-light.
The distribution of the interior is regulated in its proportions by the beautiful atrium with its four columns. Here the space is divided into three bays by the shafts of the columns, which support the impressive structure of the cross-vaulting; while the pure white walls are opened into niches with statues of the Seasons by Alessandro Vittoria. A narrow barrel-vaulted passage links the atrium with the portico facing the garden; this is flanked by the fine oval staircases. The salon is on the piano nobile, above the atrium.
The attribution to Palladio is borne out by the *Quattro Libri*. Construction was under way in September 1553 and seems to have been completed by 1555. Its conception can thus be dated to about 1552, which allows us to connect it with the all-important design of the Palazzo Chiericati (begun in 1550-1551), where Palladio introduced the loggia-on-loggia system, followed soon after by the similar Villa Cornaro at Piombino Dese. Palladio himself must have supervised construction at least in part, since his presence in the home of his client, Francesco Pisani, in Montagnana is documented in November 1553.
A comparison with the design in the treatise shows that the completed building lacks the two short service wings attached to its sides by a kind of triumphal arch straddling each roadway. The villa seems to be complete as it is, to judge from the degree of finish of the sides, with the Doric frieze running unbroken across them, and it seems likely that the service wings were unnecessary because it was not intended for the administration of large landed estates. Some scholars suggest that this was a new kind of villa connected with industrial activity, since the watercourse below it used to work watermills (formerly belonging to the Carraresi family, the feudal lords of the town), over which the Pisani family seem to have enjoyed special jurisdiction. As for the two arches of triumph, there is an interesting suggestion that they are a trace of one of the designs Palladio produced in 1564 for the new choir of the cathedral of Montagnana and never built. Be that as it may, they are clearly meant as a tribute to Francesco Pisani, who was deeply committed to the undertaking.
Recently Palladio has also been credited with the small private chapel of Santa Maria Annunciata on the north side of the villa, beyond the garden. It was erected by Francesco Pisani in 1567 and has a very simple façade, framed by four Doric pilasters supporting the pediment and with a semicircular window above the doorway in the centre.

Bibliography: Vasari, 1568, p. 530; Palladio, 1570, 1. II, p. 52; Muttoni, 1740, p. 25; Bertotti Scamozzi, 1778, pp. 18-22; Magrini, 1845, p. 79; Burger, 1909, p. 53; Pane, 1971, pp. 194 ff.; Forssman, 1965, pp. 63 ff.; Zorzi, 1965, pp. 218-224; Ackerman, 1967, pp. 58-59; Prinz, 1969, pp. 374-376; Cevese, 1973, pp. 70-73; Puppi, 1973, pp. 288-290; Kubelik, 1974, pp. 455-456; Fairbairn in Burns, 1975, p. 193; Lewis, 1981, pp. 166-167; Rigon, 1980, nos. 11-12; Muraro, 1981-1982 and 1986, pp. 200-202; C.J. Kolb, 1984; Canova, 1985, pp. 124-133; Bödefeld- Hinz, 1987, pp. 140-144; Costant, 1987, p. 79.

Villa Cornaro

Piombino Dese (Padua),
1552; attribution certain.

From Vicenza take the state highway no. 53 (towards Treviso) as far as Castelfranco Veneto. Here take the road for Venice; after Resana one comes to Piombino Dese. The villa stands near the main square of the town, on the street to its right. It can be visited from May to September between 3.30 p.m. and 6 p.m. while groups may visit it through the whole year by previous arrangement (tel. 049/9365047).

The Villa Cornaro, like the Villa Pisani at Montagnana, with which it has close affinities, is one of the group of Palladian villas whose design combines elements of the urban palace and the country house. The former is apparent in its distribution on two *piani nobili* (in addition to the semi-basement floor), and also the absence of farm buildings, which shows that it was built to project an image rather than administer an estate. But the open form, with its deep open galleries and the wings (fairly short ones) on either side, are taken from the country villas.

The building is cube-shaped with a hexastyle pronaos emerging towards the garden on the north side, facing the road. The pronaos has two superimposed loggias of the Ionic and Corinthian orders, preceded by steps. Two short wings project from the sides, markedly lower than the main block, to which they are linked by the continuation of the plinth and the trabeation of the first order. A narrow entrance passage leads into the fine hall with its four columns. Unlike the Montagnana villa, where the corresponding hall serves as an atrium, here it is the centre of the villa, "so that it is far from the heat and the cold," Palladio tells us in the *Quattro Libri*.

This room creates a serene and monumentally classical composure, and acts as the pivot around which the other rooms, of various shapes and sizes, are laid out, together with the magnificent oval staircases leading up to the first floor. Four slender Ionic columns support the coffered ceiling and the floor of the upper chamber, while the corners of the walls open into niches with stucco portraits of the owner of the villa, Giorgio Cornaro, and other members of the family, such Catherine, Queen of Cyprus, and her husband Jacopo di Lusignano. They are the work of the sculptor Camillo Mariani, active in the Veneto at the end of the Cinquecento and in Rome in the first decade of the following century.

The light streams in from the numerous windows looking onto the portico facing the back garden. The portico and loggia above repeat the pattern of the front elevation but instead of being set forward are incorporated into the body of the building, between the staircases, as at the Villa Pisani at Montagnana. All the outer walls are lined by the closely patterned stonework and the windows lack mouldings. The whole effect is one of monumentality, created in particular by the scale and magniloquence of the colonnades, and it is no accident that this villa was one of the most influential models for English and American Palladianism.

There has never been any question about the attribution of the villa, thanks to the testimony of the *Quattro Libri* and also a reference by Vasari in the *Lives* of 1568. As for its date, this has only been fixed with some certainty following the recent discovery of relevant records. We know that Giorgio Cornaro, a Venetian nobleman, began work on it in about 1553, as in October of that year the steward of the estates at Piombino started a ledger, when the main block of the new villa was already fit for habitation, though work continued all through 1554, and in July the master mason was paid for a trip to Venice to consult "messer Andrea Palladio." It is virtually certain that work came to a halt in that same year, leaving the villa only partially inhabitable and perhaps without the second order of the loggia or the wings. The heirs of Giorgio Cornaro declared it was still unfinished in 1582, though in the meantime another round of work had begun in 1569 to provide it with barns and other outhouses at some distance from it. It was only in 1588, when we have a record of the arrival of a large quantity of building material, that it seems to have taken on something of its present appearance; and this is shown in great detail in a map of 1613 (published in Puppi, 1973, p. 292). Besides, as we have seen, the statues by Camillo Mariani in the hall date from the end of the sixteenth century. The sculptor must have

Drawing of the plan and elevation of the Villa Cornaro (from the "Quattro Libri").

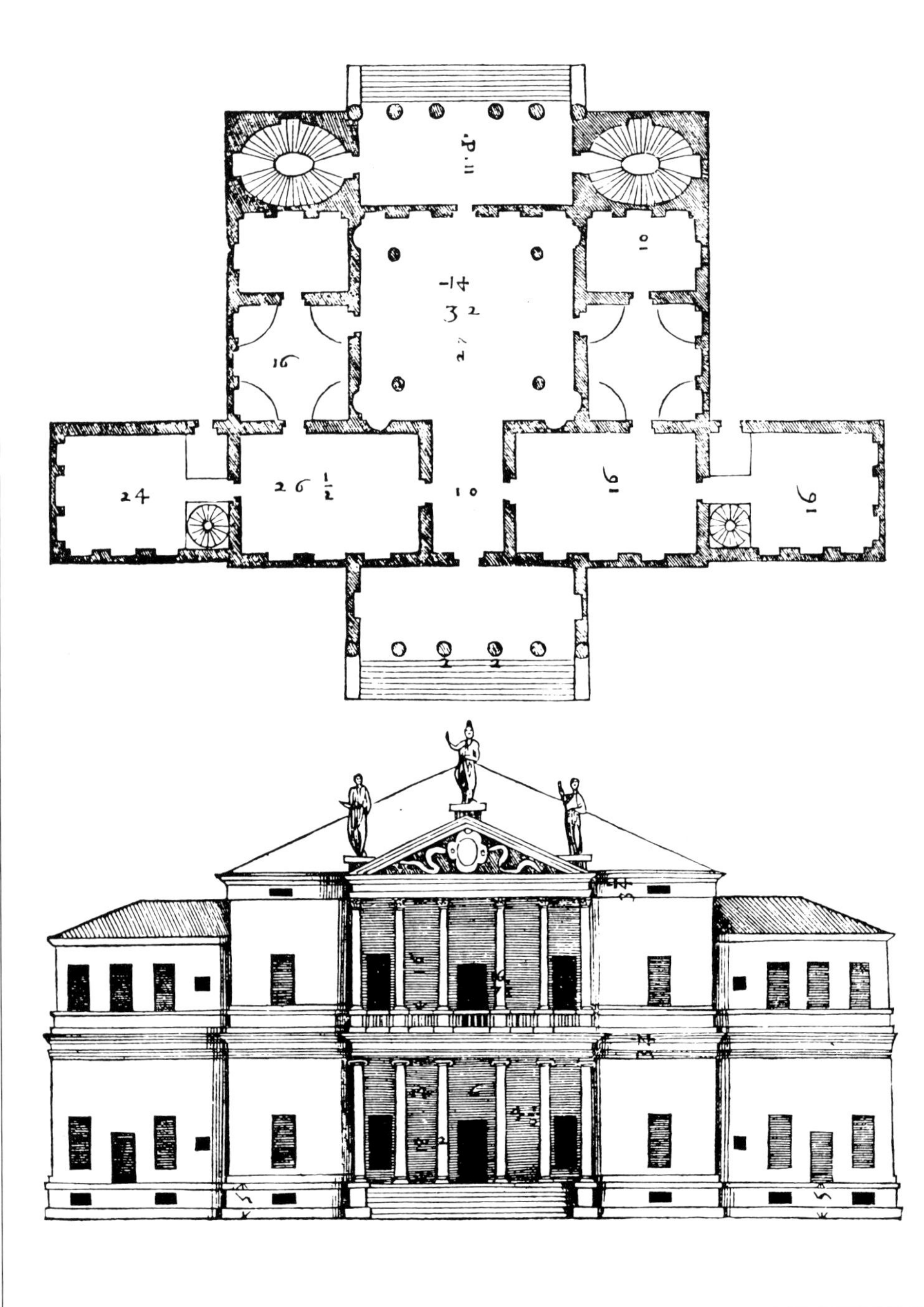

Villa Cornaro, the front elevation and chamber with the four columns.

Villa Cornaro, the statue of Caterina Cornaro by Camillo Mariani.

been summoned to the villa in 1596, when his friend, the famous architect Vincenzo Scamozzi, was also present in the house, working on the design of the great outhouse shown on the 1613 map to the right of the villa. This is still to be seen, its long northern elevation facing onto the square of the town, though the arrangement of the windows has been altered. It is even plausible that Scamozzi may have been entrusted with completing Palladio's work, as happened elsewhere.
The panels over the doors and the other stucco decorations in the villa are the work of Bartolomeo Cabianca, from the second half of the eighteenth century, when the frescoes by Mattia Bortoloni were added to the rooms at the side of the ground floor and the two smaller rooms on the upper floor, respectively depicting stories from the Old and the New Testament.

Bibliography: Vasari, 1568, p. 528; Palladio, 1570, 1. II, p. 53; Muttoni, 1740, p. 26; Bertotti Scamozzi, 1781, p. 33 ff.; Magrini, 1945, pp. 77, LXXII; Burger, 1909, pp. 95-98; Ivanoff, 1950; Pane, 1961, pp. 233 ff.; Forssman, 1965, p. 78; Ackerman, 1967, pp. 60-62; Prinz, 1969, p. 380; Zorzi, 1969, pp. 192-198; Lewis, 1972; Cevese, 1973, pp. 68-70; Puppi, 1973, pp. 292-295; Kubelik, 1974, pp. 461-462; Boucher, in Burns, 1975, pp. 194-195; Lewis 1975; Puppi, 1976; Rigon, 1980, nos. 9-10; Canova, 1985, pp. 134-147; Muraro, 1986, p. 278; Costant, 1987, pp. 75-77.

Villa Ragona

Drawing with the plan and elevation of the Villa Ragona (from the "Quattro Libri").

Ghizzolle di Montegaldella (Vicenza), 1553-1555 (?); attribution of the design certain, never built.

The precise site intended for the villa is not known. The village of Ghizzolle is between Montegaldella (to the right of the state highway joining Vicenza and Padua, near Grisignano di Zocco) and Villaganzerla.

In the *Quattro Libri* Palladio published the plan and elevation of a villa which he declared had been built by Girolamo Ragona, a gentleman of Vicenza, at Ghizzolle, near Montegaldella. The statement has bewildered scholars because there is not trace of the building, nor is there any record of it apart from the reference by Palladio. The Ragona family owned numerous properties in the area and Girolamo spent much of his time there in a mansion he owned, to which he also invited friends. Andrea may well have produced a design for alterations to this mansion, but nothing suggests that work ever began. None of the buildings once belonging to the Ragona family that still exist can be connected with the work of Palladio. All we have to go by are the drawings in the treatise, which reveal the difficulties encountered in the definition of the design, including glaring inconsistencies between the plan and the elevation. Note, for example, the awkward placing of the staircase in the middle of the house—also apparent in the design of the Villa Mocenigo at Marocco, or the uncertainty in the point of attachment of the porticoed wings at the sides of the entrance steps, while in the elevation they are set back against the sides of the residential block. The dating of the design is difficult; it can only be pointed out that there are similarities in its composition with the elevation of the Villa Thiene at Cicogna and Villa Chiericati at Vancimuglio which suggest the years around 1553-1555.

Bibliography: Palladio, 1570, 1. II, p. 57; Muttoni, 1740, pp. 29-30; Bertotti Scamozzi, 1778, p. 37; Magrini, 1845, p. 241; Burger, 1909, p. 135; Pane, 1961, p. 224; Ackerman, 1967, p. 75; Zorzi, 1969, pp. 74-77; Puppi, 1973, pp. 295-296; Canova, 1985, pp. 148-149.

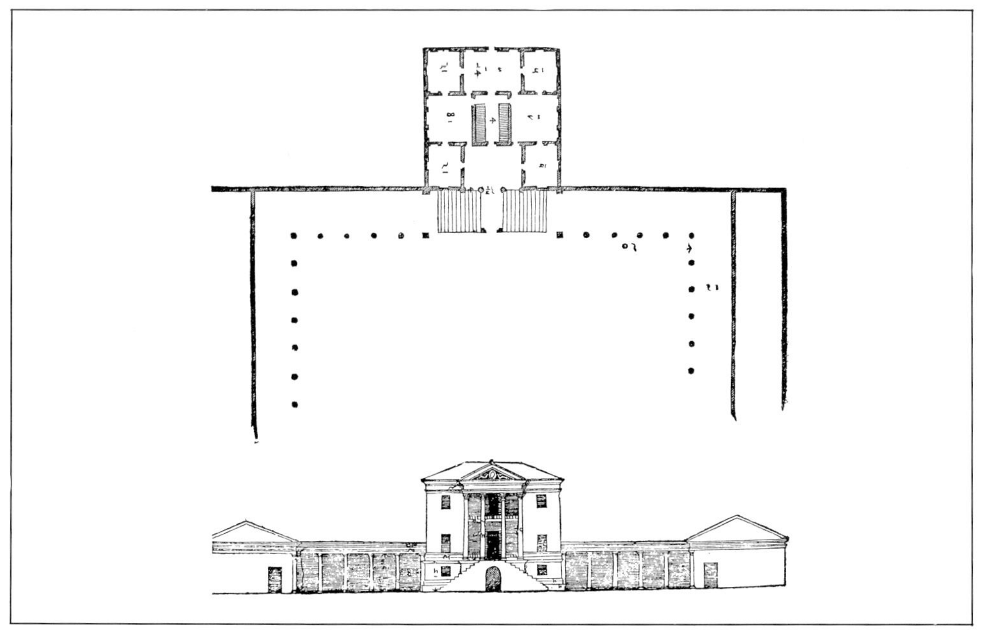

Villa Trissino

76 Meledo di Sarego (Vicenza),
1553-1554 (?); attribution of the design certain, never built.

From Vicenza take the state highway for Verona and turn left at Alte Ceccato, travelling towards Lonigo. The road passes through Meledo (before reaching Sarego), where it is flanked on the right by a canal and then a new church. Here stands the building that formerly belonged to the Trissino family, with its farm buildings and dovecotes.

On page 60 of the second volume of Palladio's *Quattro Libri* Palladio presents the plan and elevation of a spectacular villa to be built on two storeys, designed for Francesco and Ludovico Trissino, of a noble family of Vicenza, for whom he also seems to have planned an urban palace—never built—in 1558.
The design of the residence—set on a slight rise—develops (as in the Villa Almerico, better known as La Rotonda) around a circular chamber rising the full height of the building and ending in a dome. Here—as in the design for the Villa Thiene at Cicogna—the perimetre of this chamber has "a series of half-columns supporting a balcony, from which one can enter the upstairs rooms." In contrast to the crystalline geometrical purity of the Villa Rotonda, the lesser rooms are arranged awkwardly and incoherently around the great chamber. Of the four tetrastyle pronaoses set in the centre of the four sides of the building, only those at the front and back are set forward from the façades, while the side ones are incorporated into them. At the point of attachment between the staircases leading to the portico of the main elevation there are two curved colonnades each of which projects a quarter of a circle. Just below the point where they end, the porticoed outhouses stretch sideways and then form a right-angle. In his comment, Palladio also mentions the presence of two dovecotes on the bank of a river, which do not appear in the drawing. Scholars agree that the design for the Villa Trissino is derived from the design of the Rotonda as it appears in the *Quattro Libri*, and relate the centralized scheme found in both buildings to the specific features of the site. Palladio in fact says that at Meledo "the site is very fine, because it is on top of a hill washed by a pleasant river and in the middle of a spacious plain with a busy road running alongside it. The round chamber will stand on the crown of the hill..." So this is a villa conceived as if it were a belvedere, giving a wonderful view over the landscape. The curved porticoed wings clearly present similarities with the Villa Badoera at Fratta Polesine and the designs for the Villa Thiene at Cicogna and Villa Mocenigo on the Brenta. Both the centralized design and the circular porticoes seem to derive from reflection on the complex acropolises of the ancients, such as the temple of Hercules at Tivoli and the temple of Fortuna at Palestrina, reconstructed conjecturally by Palladio on a number of occasions. The most likely date for the Meledo design, especially the residential section, seems to be the later 1560s, after the design for the Villa Almerico. Against this is the fact that the commission was first requested before 1562, the year before the death of Ludovico Trissino, who commissioned it with his brother Francesco. As with other designs in the *Quattro Libri*, which are similarly complex, difficult to build (if only because of the cost) and at best only partially completed, this project raises the question of whether it was ever really submitted to the clients. The same problem arises with the Villa Mocenigo on the Brenta and it also existed the Villa Thiene at Quinto Vicentino until the actual working drawings were found and proved to be far simpler and more realistic. So the case at Meledo may well be the same: the initial idea for the villa was more practicable but it was left unbuilt, so Palladio revised and developed it for publication.
We can now take the evidence provided by the archives and a long series of maps (see Kubelik, 1974, pp. 449-451 and Puppi, 1974, pp. 93-96) to see just what was actually built at Meledo in those years. The site intended for the villa is at present occupied by an old Quattrocento house on a slight rise alongside the new village church, with two porticoed farm buildings with Tuscan columns at the corners of a lower courtyard. The building with the stream called the Brendola running past it at the back is set markedly forward in relation to the other. In front of this there is a dovecote joined to a wall with a low gateway

Drawing with the plan and elevation of the Villa Trissino (from the "Quattro Libri").

framed by rustic stonework of unusual workmanship.

Between August 1553 and January 1554 we know that work was going ahead on a dovecote, a surrounding wall for what was called the upper courtyard, and a gate. A map of 1569 shows that the wall was to surround a large rectangular courtyard which also comprised the Quattrocento building, while the dovecote must have been the one shown as attached to a porticoed building which, as far as one can tell, was the one on the left. Before its destruction in the last century this dovecote bore the date 1576, which may refer to a later restructuring. The present dovecote on the river appears only on a map from the late sixteenth century, and the date of construction is in fact 1575, as shown by the date carved on the exterior with the initials F.T. (Francesco Trissino). The windows are of different shapes and badly arranged, so that it is not easy to see Palladio's hand in the building, unless it was built without his direct supervision by unskilful workmen. For a period it must actually have served as a residence for the owners, since the ground floor rooms were decorated with grotesques in 1576, which are now almost impossible to make out (the painter may have been Bernardino India or Eliodoro Forbicini) and there is also a fine marble fireplace. A surprising item appears in maps from 1662-1663: six Tuscan columns laid out in a row parallel to the river, starting from the dovecote on the right. They are free-standing columns, without a building behind them, and remained like this until soon after 1740 when the outhouse was completed. To conclude, it seems that a start was made at restructuring the farm buildings at Meledo in about 1553-1554. Palladio's design may already have been available, though we know nothing about it, but it could have included the curv-

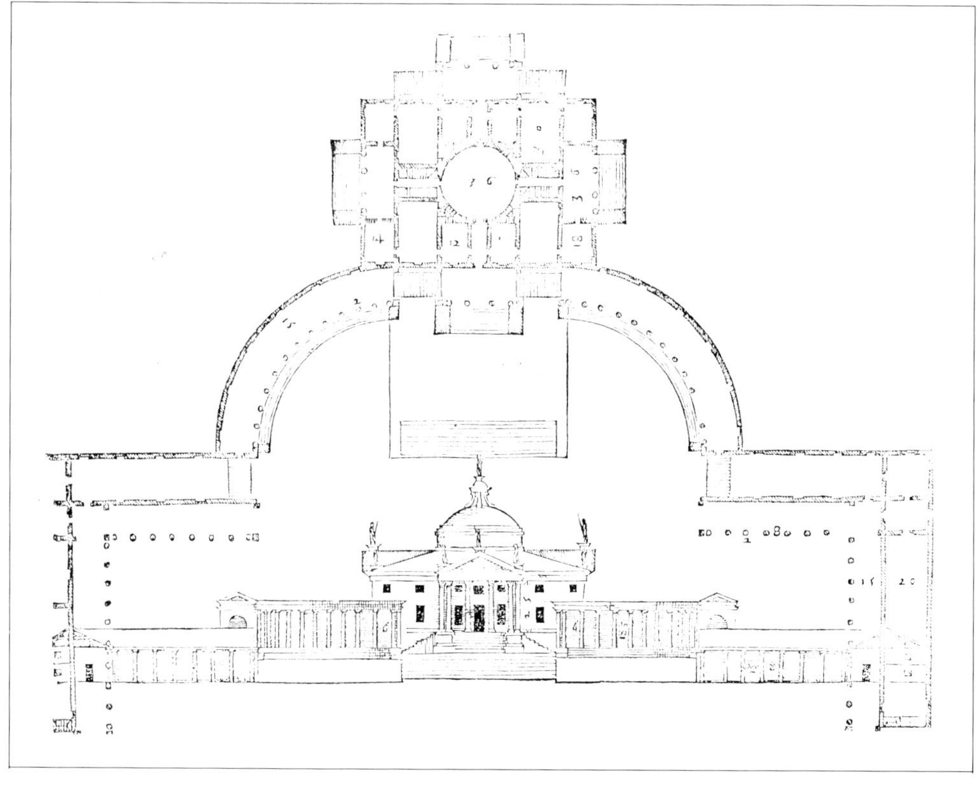

Villa Trissino, view of the complex with the outhouses and dovecote now on the site assigned to the villa.

ing colonnades experimented with at about the same time in the Villa Badoer at Fratta Polesine and the Villa Thiene at Cicogna.
At any rate, the work stopped with the death of Ludovico Trissino in 1562, when the courtyard had been defined and a dovecote built, annexed to the present outhouse on the left, which may also have been completed. The design had no sequel, save, perhaps, for the hyperbolical elaboration of it that we find in the treatise in 1570. Five years later Francesco Trissino seems to have tried to revive the project, getting no further than the construction and decoration of the dovecote on the right. The work carried out in the next two centuries seems to have been much more ambitious, an attempt to imitate the illustration in the *Quattro Libri*, perhaps by using columns which had been prepared in the sixteenth century so that these would be all that remains of Palladio at Meledo.

Bibliography: Vasari, 1568, p. 528; Palladio, 1570, 1. II, p. 60; Muttoni, 1740, p. 34; Bertotti Scamozzi, 1781, pp. 12-13; Magrini, 1845, p. 245; Burger, 1909, pp. 112-118; Pane, 1961, pp. 191-194; Forssman, 1965, p. 54; Ackerman, 1967, p. 77; Isermeyer, 1967, p. 209; Zorzi, 1969, pp. 143-151; Cevese, 1971, II, p. 587 and 1973, pp. 65-68; Puppi, 1973, pp. 385-388 and 1974, pp. 93-96; Kubelik, 1974, pp. 449-451; Burns, 1975, pp. 250-251; Gioseffi, 1978, pp. 38-45; Costant, 1987, pp. 99-100.

Villa Mocenigo "sopra la Brenta"

Dolo (Venice),
1554 (?) and 1560; attribution certain, altered and then demolished.

The site of this villa lies at Pecora, on the left bank of the Brenta canal. It can be reached by taking the state highway that runs from Padua towards Venice. Pecora is between Fiesso d'Artico and Paluello.

The site "on the Brenta" in a property belonging to the *cavaliere* Leonardo Mocenigo (for whom Palladio states the villa complex illustrated in the second of the *Quattro Libri* was designed) has been accurately identified on the basis of records. It lies in an area comprised within the southern bend of the waterway between Dolo and Paluello, near Fiesso d'Artico. The same researches have shown that a number of building projects followed one another here all through the Cinquecento but we are unable to determine their exact scope, so the history of the building, demolished in 1835, is blurred, and there is no way of knowing how far it corresponded to the drawing in the treatise.

Design for the Villa Mocenigo "sopra la Brenta" (London, R.I.B.A., XVI, 2).

The client, Leonardo Mocenigo, of the branch of the "zogie" (i.e. pearls) was a great lover of antiques, a collector of archaeological relics and deeply committed to the celebration of his own standing as a cultivated aristocrat, which he effected by renewing the various residences he inherited in classical style. His relationship with Palladio was close, and led to several commissions: in addition to the villa on the Brenta, there was the villa for Marocco in 1561-1562, the remodelling of the house in Sant'Eufemia in Padua in 1558-1561, the family chapel in the church of Santa Lucia (later destroyed) in Venice, and the ebony chest in the form of the Arch of Constantine to contain his collection of coins (now lost).
It is possible that the first commission at Dolo goes back to as early as 1554. The documents do not mention the architect's name but show that at the start of that year Mocenigo ordered the purchase and preparation of the stones needed for a "building at Dolo." At any rate, whatever the purpose, this project would have had to reckon with the buildings already on the site. In the 1520s and '30s his grandfather, Alvise Mocenigo, had reclaimed

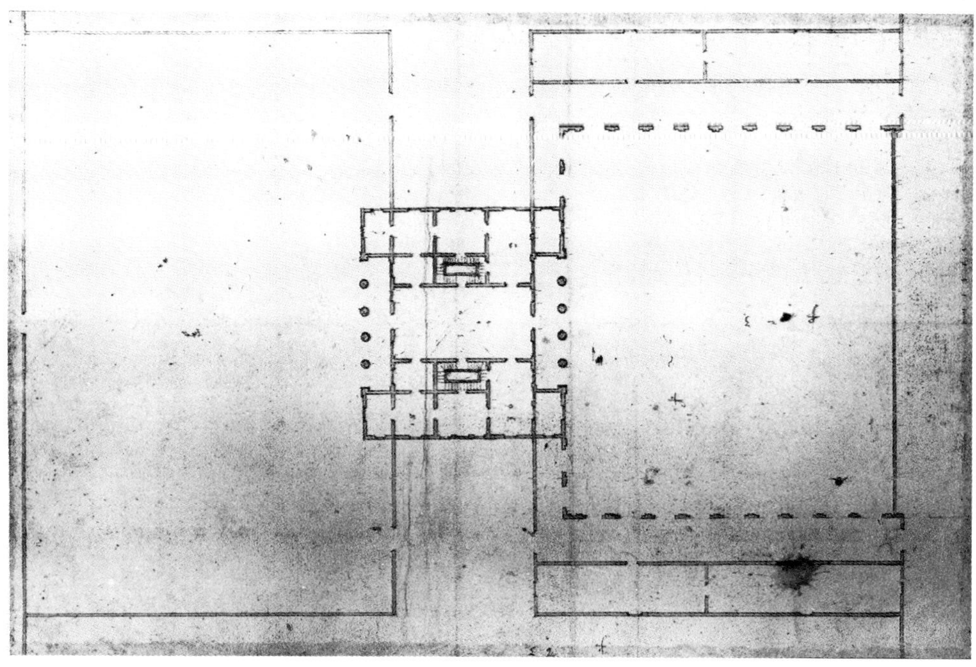

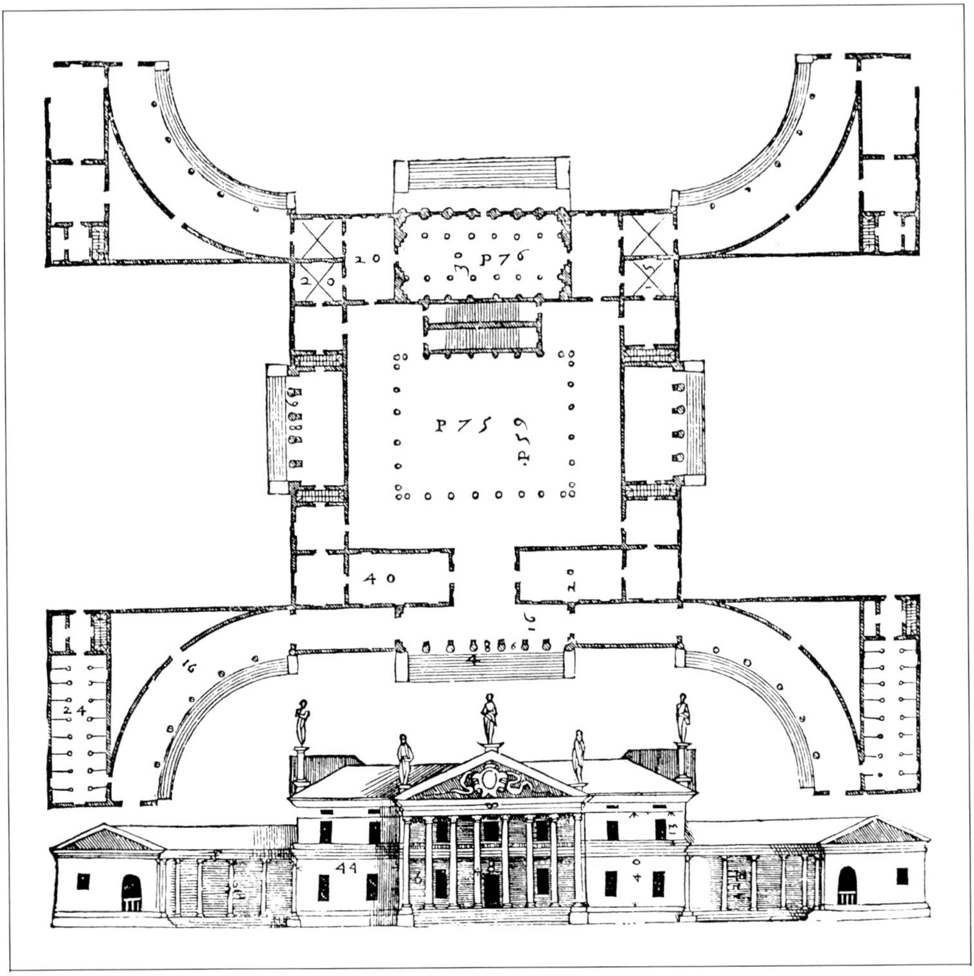

Drawing with the plan and elevation of the Villa Mocenigo "sopra la Brenta" (from the "Quattro Libri").

a large area of land in the area, providing the necessary structures for running the estate and a residence for himself. There is no sign that his grandson intended to demolish it. So in this state of affairs he must have been simply refurbishing the old house, perhaps with a more modern exterior to fit the canons of classical architecture. The supply of dressed stone may even have been meant for the construction of outhouses. We know nothing more about it.

After 1554 there seems to have been no construction work, but it began again in 1560, when Mocenigo returned from Germany, where he had gone as ambassador of the Serenissima between 1557 and 1559. This time Palladio's presence is borne out by the records. Following his designs, the capitals of four columns were cut, followed by the supply of modillions, eight door-frames, etc. A ledger opened in September 1562 and closed in March 1564 records that the interior of the building was being fitted up, and shows that once more it was a refurbishing of the old house, as appears from references to the demolition and alterations made to walls.

There is no record of the results of this second bout of restoration work (it might have been the continuation of the 1564 operation). But given the small number of columns prepared, we can rule out the likelihood that it was an even partial construction of the design in the *Quattro Libri*. The latter shows an enormous, rectangular residence laid out around a colonnaded peristyle. At the centre of each side is a double loggia screened by a single order of giant columns supporting the pediment. Two semicircular colonnades stretch away from the sides of the main elevations, masking the outbuildings. The whole forms a complex architectural "machine," costly and difficult to build, which brings us back to the insistent problem of the reliability of the engravings in the treatise as a guide to the designs actually submitted to Palladio's clients. This is a case in point. The project completed in 1564 seems closer to an autograph drawing generally regarded as the starting point for the more elaborate design published in 1570 (London, R.I.B.A., XVI, 2). It shows a complex with two opposed rectangular courts, only one of which is porticoed, and a residential block which opens out at the centre of the front elevation into a loggia screened by four columns. The layout of the interior is divided up by a salon that runs down the middle of the building, an arrangement well suited to an adaptation of an earlier building of the kind which is most common in the Veneto region.

Unfortunately the later history of the building, down to its demolition in 1835, makes it impossible to verify this theory. After the death of Leonardo Mocenigo during the plague of 1576, his son Alvise ordered a wholesale renewal of the whole building, even adding another storey to it, and the eighteenth century engravings consequently show a structure which has lost all traces of Palladianism.

An appraisal of the idea published in the *Quattro Libri* can be supplemented by a whole dossier of autograph drawings—starting from the one already cited—which show the development of the structure down to the final design (London, R.I.B.A., XVI, 1 and X, 1v, 2r). These show that it constitutes a return to Palladio's study of late Roman architecture, a revival of the house of the Ancient Romans, having affinities in its spatial organization with the Villa Thiene at Quinto, the Villa Trissino at Meledo and the Villa Sarego at Santa Sofia di Pedemonte. There are also evident similarities with the Villa Thiene at Cicogna and Badoer at Fratta, in the curving pattern of the outbuildings and the way they lock into the pronaos. Here Palladio was drawing on his studies of ancient temple complexes, like that of Hercules Victor at Tivoli, and also his reflections on more recent architecture in Rome, from the Villa Madama to the work of Vignola and Pirro Ligorio.

Bibliography: Palladio, 1570, 1. II, p. 66 (but 78); Muttoni, 1740, p. 17; Bertotti Scamozzi, 1783, p. 56; Gallo, 1955, pp. 29-34; Pane, 1961, pp. 272-275; Forssman, 1965, pp. 58 ff.; Ackerman, 1967, p. 79; Zorzi, 1969, pp. 90-94; Puppi, 1973, pp. 358-361; Burns, 1975, p. 223; Guiotto, 1980, pp. 140-143; Lewis, 1981, pp. 98-100 and 124-128; Bassi, 1987, pp. 388-391; Puppi, 1987.

Villa Barbaro

82 Maser (Treviso),
1554; attribution certain.

From Bassano del Grappa take the road towards Montebelluna. Where the road climbs up towards Asolo take the turn-off for Cornuda. The villa is on the far side of the town of Maser. It can be visited on Tuesday, Saturday, Sunday and public holidays. June-September, 3 p.m.-6 p.m.; October-March, 2 p.m.-5 p.m. At other times, for groups of over ten people, phone for a booking (tel. 0423/565002).

After the Rotonda this is the most famous of Palladio's villas. A decisive contribution to its success comes from the fresco cycle it contains, the masterpiece of Paolo Veronese and Cinquecento Venetian painting, and also its marvellous position among the hills of the Trevigiano. Then there is the touch of mystery created by Palladio himself, who, in his description of the villa in the *Quattro Libri* "forgot" (though generally attentive to such details) to mention the name of the celebrated artist who decorated it, giving rise to a flurry of conjectures about his possible dislike of the spatial distortions in Veronese's frescoes.
The problems raised by the building go far beyond this strange silence and even call in question the actual extent of Andrea's responsibility for the present complex, the nature of the structures already on the site and the degree to which his clients, the Barbaro brothers (figures of some importance), intervened in the definition of the design. Marcantonio Barbaro was a lover of architecture and an amateur sculptor; Daniele (designated by the Patriarch of Aquileia to be his successor) was a student of perspective and the works of Vitruvius. In 1556 he published a translation and commentary of the *Ten Books of Architecture* in collaboration with Palladio, who also provided some of the drawings. So both were qualified to contribute actively to the design of the villa. Besides, scholars have noted here a number of incongruities, unusual features and ambiguities in the relation between decoration and architecture, all of which can only be imputed to interference by the clients and also—as we shall see—the constraints imposed by earlier structures and the hand of Veronese.

The Palladian edifice is the outcome of the brilliant restructuring of an old manor house which had long been in the Barbaro family. The earlier building can be seen in the section of the present residence that emerges from the line of the porticoed outbuildings. This appears from certain features discovered during recent restoration work: bricked-up windows, traces of old coffered ceilings above the vaulting, beams in the outbuildings showing they were originally detached structures. Moreover the old house must have seemed perfectly adequate to Francesco, the father of Marcantonio and Daniele, because we know that the painters Giambattista Ponchini (a native of Castelfranco Veneto but educated at Rome in the School of Michelangelo) and the youthful Girolamo Mazzoni of Brescia (later very successful in Rome as a landscape-painter) were brought there in 1548, presumably to decorate it. His sons naturally did not share this opinion, as was inevitable, given their interest in classical architecture. So nothing is more likely than that Daniele in particular, who seems to have played the leading role in the matter, desired to apply his studies of Vitruvius and the houses of the ancients, and so decided to call in Palladio, whom he knew well and had worked with since at least 1550. It is not clear exactly when this decision was taken; but in the early 1550s, after the death of their father, the brothers certainly engaged in large-scale reorganization of their estates at Maser, while the site of the manor house was completely enclosed. The final design must have been drawn up after Palladio and Daniele Barbaro returned from their trip to Rome which lasted from February to June 1554, perhaps with the aim of verifying in practice the theoretical studies on which they were engaged. The invention of the very fine semicircular nymphaeum, set in the hillside at the back of the house, level with the *piano nobile*, presupposes an encounter with Pirro Ligorio, who had been working on the gardens of the Villa d'Este at Tivoli since 1550, as well as a knowledge of the ground plans of the Villa Madama and Villa Giulia, not yet completed but already at the centre of architectural debate. The hemicyclical fountain at Maser is unparalleled in Palladio's work, so that some scholars attribute it to Daniele alone, though a col-

Drawing with the plan and elevation of the Villa Barbaro (from the "Quattro Libri").

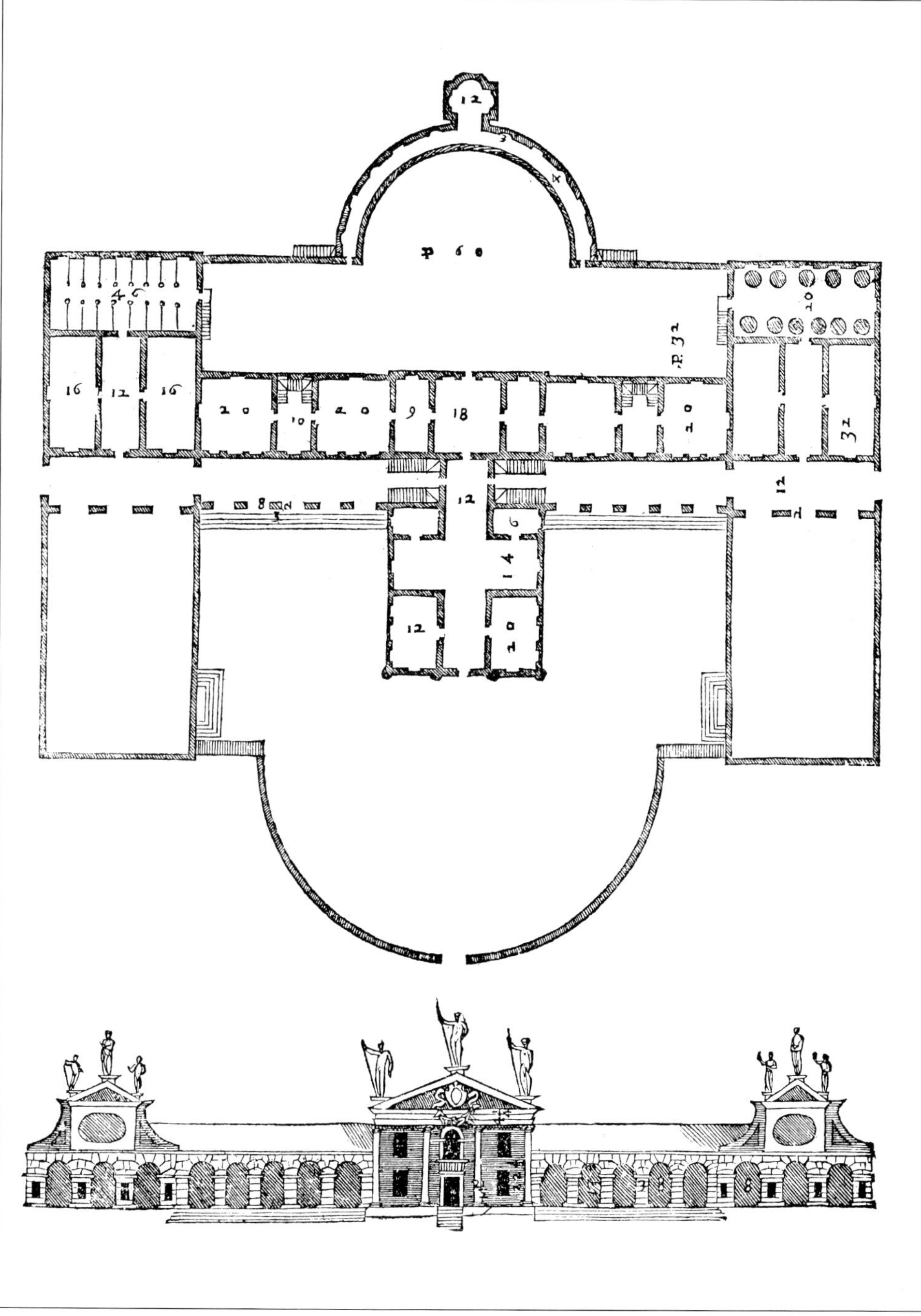

Villa Barbaro, view of the front and the nymphaeum.

laboration between the two seems more likely. But it is not at all improbable that the great statues that adorn it, generally attributed to Alessandro Vittoria and his workshop, are actually by the dilettante Marcantonio Barbaro. They represent the divinities of Olympus, each identified by an epigram, and are set in niches in the curved wall, closely decorated with trophies and festoons and framed by imposing telamons supporting the base of the pediment. In the centre, where the water wells out, an arch leads into a grotto once wholly frescoed by Veronese with an Allegory of Venice in the guise of a woman crowned and with the lion of St. Mark by her side.

It seems that the need to link the splendid nymphaeum visually with the villa explains the unusually deep body of the latter. This design shows once more Palladio's remarkable ability to adapt his ideas to the "accidental" qualities of a given site. While retaining the outer structure of the old house he added the rear section, comprising the room known as the "Chamber of Olympus" and two others at the sides, so providing a link with the formerly isolated outbuildings. The layout of the *piano nobile* is also unusual: it develops along a conceptual line that runs from the balcony in the façade into the cruciform chamber flooded with light from the wings on either side, then crosses the Chamber of Olympus and so reaches the "secret garden" of the nymphaeum. This development in unusual depth is combined with the transversal line that runs from the stairs to the *piano nobile* along the porticoes of the outbuildings, screened by the severe arcading borne on pillars and terminating in the highly imaginative and unusual dovecotes. The latter are decorated with niches containing statues, masks on the keystones of the vaulting, and sundials.

The presence of building workers in the Villa Barbaro in 1554-1555 shows that work was going ahead then. It must have been completed by 1558 when it was mentioned in a poem by the writer Magagnò of Vicenza, while the celebrated fountain was praised in a letter by Giulia da Ponte published in 1559.

The doubts of scholars centre on the elevations of the central block. They point to the uncertainty of the apertures at the sides, which are very modest, and above all the façade. This has four Ionic semi-columns of a giant order framing all the other elements, within which the tympanums of the upper windows touch the trabeation, while the archivolt of the central balcony infringes on the base of the pediment, which is overcharged with ornament.

What can be the cause? The latest interpretations suggest that once the plan of the villa had been laid out, there were differences between Palladio and Daniele Barbaro on the very concept of the architectural work; the latter, desiring to recreate at Maser the house of the Ancients and make it a temple of Universal Harmony, meant it to represent an ideal union of all the arts, through full use of sculptural and pictorial ornament, to a degree that Palladio failed to approve of, being a convinced supporter of the primacy of architecture. It is suggested that this led to the voluntary withdrawal of Palladio and his replacement by Paolo Veronese—who had trained as an architect when young—to coordinate the final stages of construction: preparation of the interiors and the design of the doorways, fireplaces, stuccoes—perhaps produced by Alessandro Vittoria, with the help of Marcantonio Barbaro—the redefinition of Palladio's façade and finally the frescoes. So Palladio's strange silence in the *Quattro Libri* may not be his reaction to an over-exuberant painter—whom he praises elsewhere—but to a rival "architect," and at the same time as he reclaims the Villa Barbaro as his own conception he also corrects the errors in its façade in the published design.

We are unable to say when the replacement came about, but it is on record that in 1557, when the plague was raging in Venice, Paolo Veronese spent a long period with the Barbaro family at Maser. Once the rooms had been prepared, the painter would then have started on the frescoes, generally dated to 1559-1560, with final touches in the summer of 1562 when the artist's investment of large sums of money in land can be connected with the final payment for his work at the villa.

Veronese's frescoes transfigure the interiors of the villa with the brilliance of light and colour, rivalling those of the countryside glimpsed from the windows. New illusory spaces are opened up by the artist's brush;

colonnades stretching into landscapes studded with ruins or fantastic villas, doors half-open and parapets with figures resting on them, seeming to smile down on our astonishment; vaults breaking open to reveal clear skies and all the divinities of Olympus; real figures, whether scared or profane. All rendered with a light, rapid, touch, a flowing brush that seems to have worked without laboured preparation or second thoughts, creating a feast for the eyes and the spirit. The meaning of the cycle of paintings, unquestionably worked out between the artist and his patron through close discussion, has been the subject of many conjectures. Essentially it is intended to celebrate the Barbaro family, the fortunate owners and inhabitants of the villa.

The walls of the great cruciform chamber are framed by architectural motifs, either painted or stuccoed; the panels they form are decorated with landscapes (in the longer arms of the room) and niches, with unforgettable figures of musicians (in the shorter arms). There are two false doorways, with here a child emerging, and there a page, while pennons and halberds are shown lying carelessly against the Corinthian columns. The vault, now blank, was once decorated with vines and foliage. The south rooms, towards the façade, were intended as reception and dining rooms. The ceiling of the room on the right (as one comes from the salon) has a boldly foreshortened view of Bacchus revealing the mystery of wine to men. The walls are decorated with landscapes and monochrome statues in niches, while a frieze of trompe l'oeil cameos runs round the whole room. Above the fine mantelpiece (as in the other rooms) there is a fresco of Ceres and Pluto, and on the op-

Villa Barbaro, mantelpiece in one of the rooms to the south.

Villa Barbaro, vault of the Chamber of Olympus, with frescoes by Paolo Veronese.

posite wall, above the door, an Allegory of Venus and Love. The second room is devoted to the themes of love and harmony. Within a similar framework three maidens are shown intently playing stringed instruments, while the ceiling presents the Allegory of the Happy Spouses in a whirl of festive *putti*. The space above the door presents the Abundance of the Villa Barbaro in the guise of a buxom nurse busily polishing silver chalices bearing the family crest. The most significant and complex subject of the whole fresco cycle is in the chamber of Olympus, the heart of the house, which links the cruciform salon with the rear garden and nymphaeum, dividing the private rooms on either side. Here Corinthian columns on the walls frame views of landscapes and support a parapet on which lean the mistress of the house, Giustiniana Giustiniani, the wife of Marcantonio, with her nurse and youngest child, while her elder children, Almorò and Francesco are also

Villa Barbaro, the Tempietto, view of the exterior with the pronaos.

shown, the one reading and the other playing with a dog. In the lunettes the subject is the Seasons, that representing Summer being especially magnificent, while smaller panels in the ceiling present mysterious astrological symbols and enclose the central octagon, depicting the gods of Olympus set in a circle around an enigmatic female figure, borne on a dragon within a radiant halo.

To the right of the big window we find the curious depiction of the villa itself, set in a hilly landscape; it can be interpreted both as a tribute to Veronese's patrons and as an ironical claim by the painter to his part in its design. The room on the left of the chamber of Olympus is commonly called the "Chamber of the Dog" after the delightful little dog sitting by the illusionistic window opening onto a sea-

scape. Other landscapes—perhaps the least effective in the cycle—cover the walls, framed within architectural elements. Above the painted mouldings there are allegorical figures and the vault depicts a Strength seizing a cornucopia from the hands of Fortune, heedless of the snares of Envy. The lunette opposite the window presents the Holy Family, St. Catherine and St. Giovannino. The decorative scheme is repeated in the right-hand room; known also as the "Chamber of the Lamp," after the cupid holding a lighted lamp over the *Madonna della pappa* painted within a sea-shell in the lunette opposite the window. Here, too, allegorical figures rise from the moulding, and the ceiling depicts Faith and Charity. The other side-rooms do not contain frescoes, but through the doorways, on the end wall of the last room on each side, there are two paintings, framed by trompe l'oeil windows: a hunter with his dogs and a woman with a fan, traditionally reputed to be the self-portrait of the artist and his favourite model.
Relations between Palladio, the Barbaro brothers and Paolo Veronese did not deteriorate after this episode. Andrea worked again with the painter and received Marcantonio's patronage for many of his Venetian projects. Indeed, after the death of his brother, Marcantonio invited Palladio back to Maser in 1580 to work on the chapel belonging to the villa but set outside its boundaries to form the visual conclusion of the road leading from the village. Here the architect was finally able to experiment with a circular plan, which he considered the most suitable for a church, an opinion which his patron also put forward vigorously during the debate over the model to be adopted at the church of the Redentore in Venice. Naturally he supported this view with reference to the celebrated Pantheon in Rome. This design repeats the motif of the pronaos set well forward (typical of the Pantheon) above which rise two small bell towers. Palladio was now close to death, which followed in August of the same year while he was still at Maser, and he never lived to see the completion of this building, which bears his name carved on the base of the pediment. He can hardly have been responsible for the conception of the richly decorated interior. The temple was first dedicated to the Redeemer and later to Saints Paul and Andrew, the patron saints of Maser. The richness of its learned and symbolical significances make it a remarkable monument to the memory of this unique family of humanists.

Bibliography: Vasari, 1568, p. 530; Palladio, 1570, 1. II, p. 51; Muttoni, 1740, p. 24; Bertotti Scamozzi, 1781, pp. 26-29; Magrini, 1845, pp. 77, LXXII, 218; Burger, 1909, pp. 101-110; AA.VV., 1960; Ivanoff, 1961; Pane, 1961, pp. 29, 235 ff.; Cessi, 1964; Wittkower, 1964, pp. 131-132; Forssman, 1965, pp. 72 ff.; Ackerman, 1967, pp. 56-58; Basso, 1968; Oberhuber, 1968; Wolters, 1968, pp. 262-264; Zorzi, 1969, pp. 169-181; Ivanoff, 1970; Cocke, 1972; Cevese, 1973, pp. 78-81; Lewis, 1973; Puppi, 1973, pp. 314-318; Huse, 1974; Kubelik, 1974, pp. 456-457; Burns, 1975, p. 196; Basso, 1976; Pignatti, 1976, I, pp. 56-68; Oechslin, 1977; Burns, 1979 (II), pp. 128-136; Lewis, 1980; Rigon, 1980, nos. 15-18; Puppi, 1980 (II); Puttfarken, 1980; Lewis, 1981, pp. 157-158; Marder, 1981; Crosato Larcher, 1982; Battilotti-Puppi, 1973; Azzi Visentini, 1984, pp. 152 ff.; Battilotti, 1985; Canova, 1985, pp. 167-185; Murato, 1986, pp. 210-239; Bödefeld-Hinz, 1987, pp. 144-147; Costant, 1987, pp. 73-74.

Villa Barbaro, the Tempietto, view of the interior.

Villa Chiericati Porto

90 Vancimuglio di Grumolo delle Abbadesse (Vicenza),
1554-1555; attribution not certain.

Vancimuglio stands on the state highway no. 11 between Vicenza and Padua. The gate of the villa opens directly onto the road, on the left-hand side.

The attribution to Palladio of this villa, not recorded in the *Quattro Libri*, has divided the scholars. The majority seem to accept it, with qualifications. There is an autograph plan (London, R.I.B.A., XVI, 20) referring to it, which seems to clear away all reasonable doubts about Palladio's responsibility for the design. There is also the fact that the client was Giovanni Chiericati, the brother of Girolamo Chiericati who commissioned Palladio to design the *palazzo* in Piazza Matteotti in Vicenza in 1550-1551. However the long and troubled history of its construction, over which Palladio had no control, was the cause of the mistakes and alterations that depart from the original plan.
We learn from Giovanni Chiericati's will in 1557 that the villa was still being built, so the design and start of work must precede that date but be later than 1554, when a declaration to the fiscal office in Vicenza showed that there were only two older buildings on the site. Building must have come to a halt very early, at the latest at the foundations, because in a map of 1562 (published by Puppi, 1974, pp. 102-103) the surveyors—normally very accurate—only recorded two farm buildings. Little had been added two years later, when Giovanni's son Lionello declared to the fiscal office the existence of an uninhabited house, without floors or windows and with only the outline of the main hall and bedrooms. The building was only completed by the next owner, Ludovico Porto (following his purchase of the property in 1574) at some time before 1584.
The most glaring deviation from the original plan concerns the central chamber. The architect developed scheme very close to the design of the ground floor at the Palazzo Chiericati, with the variations he had worked out for the Villa Pisani at Bagnolo, to produce a highly imaginative biapsidal interior, cross-vaulted and enlivened by niches and recesses. The present room is instead a large, plain cube-shaped space, with a beamed ceiling. The change in plan led to the closure of the thermal window, initially set above the door in the rear façade and naturally linked to a vaulted room; but it proved useless when the flat ceiling reduced it to a window in the loft. The other rooms retain the harmony of proportions typical of Palladio; the two large rectangular rooms at the sides of the narrow entrance passage are especially elegant.
The façade displays evident errors in the placing of the windows and the way the staircase has been restricted to the central intercolumn. It has the classical pronaos set slightly forward from the rest of the building, a detail introduced earlier at Piombino Dese; here, instead, it is a tetrastyle instead of hexastyle, and its verticalism is accentuated by the giant order of Ionic columns, a scheme adopted on a number of subsequent occasions. The rear elevation, articulated only by the slight projection of the middle section and its tympanum, looks rather awkward because of the numerous windows of various shapes set in it.
The outhouse now resting against the right side of the villa is an eighteenth century addition.

Bibliography: Bertotti Scamozzi, 1781, pp. 48-49; Magrini, 1845, p. 289; Burger, 1909, p. 52; Dalla Pozza, 1943, pp. 156-164 and 1943-1963, pp. 121-131; Pane, 1961, p. 225; Ackerman, 1967, pp. 72-73; Zorzi, 1969, pp. 156-160; Cevese, 1971, II, p. 428; Lewis, 1973, p. 371 and pp. 377-378, no. 13; Puppi, 1973, pp. 296-297 1974, pp. 102-103; Fairbairn, in Burns, 1975, p. 195; Lewis, 1981, pp. 152-154; Costant, 1987, pp. 59-60.

Design of Villa Chiericati Porto (London, R.I.B.A., XVI, 20).

Villa Chiericati Porto, front elevation.

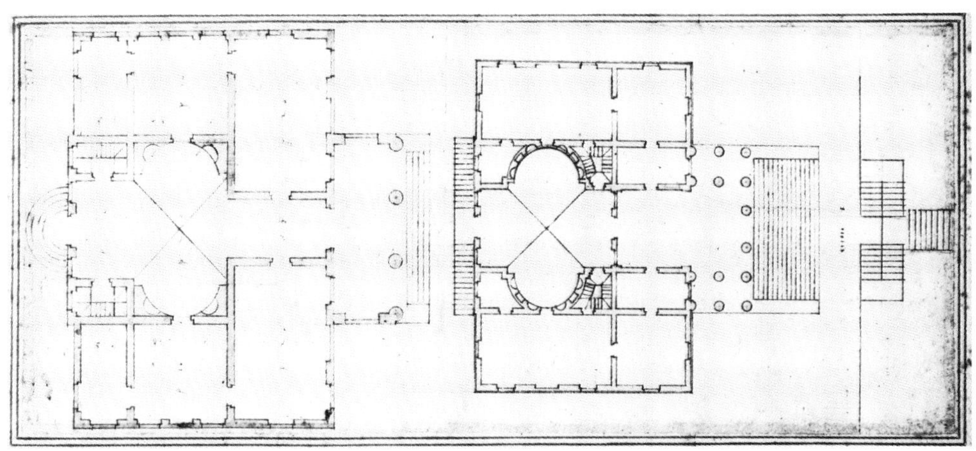

Villa Porto (Vivaro), view of the whole.

92 Vivaro di Dueville (Vicenza), 1554 (?); attribution not certain.

Take the state highway from Vicenza in the direction of Bassano del Grappa. After Polegge, turn left for Vivaro; the road curves in a large arc and leads to the villa.

This house is similar in type to the Villa Chiericati, Having a tetrastyle pronaos with giant Ionic columns set forward from the line of the façade, preceded by a tall staircase; the pronaos comprises the two upper storeys of the buildings. Some scholars see it—with reservations—as designed by Palladio, naturally with reference only to the central body of thepresent spectacular complex, the wings having been added in the mid-nineteenth century by the architect Antonio Caregaro Negrin, who drew on the illustration of the Villa Pisani at Montagnana in the *Quattro Libri*. The same intervention marred the rear elevation of the Cinquecento building, obscured the front, and altered part of the interior. The parts that remained untouched were the ground floor rooms, with their fine segmented vaulting, and the splendid salon on the *piano nobile*, with its ceiling of wooden beams. The other rooms are laid out at its sides, in a scheme dear to Palladio.

The uncertainty over the attribution of this building stems largely from the almost complete absence of records providing the name of the person that commissioned it and its chronology. A date, however approximate, would prove very useful, because in the mid-sixteenth century the pronaos, borrowed from the classical temple and applied to a secular building, was found only in Palladio's works, but by the century's end it had become fairly common, being used by his imitators. The little information we possess here suggests a date before the middle of the 1550s, which would mean the design must have been by Palladio. This villa might be the same as the manor house, valued at the substantial figure of 900 ducats, reported to the tax authorities in 1554 by its noble owner, Paolo Porto (supposing him to have been the client). This theory seems confirmed by the recent discovery, during restoration work, of Cinquecento frescoes under the windows of the salon, which some scholars identify as the work of Giallo Fiorentino from the period between 1555 and 1565. This was the same painter that had worked in about 1558 on the Villa Badoer and 1564 on the Villa Grimaldi in Fratta Polesine, the former definitely by Palladio and the other attributed to him.

Bibliography: Dalla Pozza, 1943, p. 410; Zorzi, 1969, p. 226; Cevese, 1971, II, p. 410; Puppi, 1973, pp. 297-298; Tiozzo, 1981, p. 41.

Villa Badoer, known as "La Badoera"

Fratta Polesine (Rovigo),
1555; attribution certain.

Take the road from Rovigo towards Badia Polesine. Turn left for Fratta before reaching Lendinara. The villa faces the town square from the other side of the canal. It can be visited from 15 September to 30 March every day, 2 p.m.-5 p.m.; from 1 April to 14 September every day, 3.30 p.m.-7 p.m.; from 16 April to 30 September on Sundays, 10 a.m.-12 a.m. On Thursday all the year round, 9. a.m.-12 a.m. and Tuesday from 15 September to 15 June, 9. a.m.-12 a.m. (tel. 0425/68122).

This is indisputably one of the finest of Palladio's villas, displaying the full maturity of his powers. Included in the *Quattro Libri* and mentioned by Vasari in his *Lives* in 1568, its history is also clear, thanks to assiduous research in the archives and the discovery of useful maps.
The client, Palladio tells us, was the Venetian nobleman Francesco Badoer; he possessed vast estates—though they were on marshy land and not particularly profitable—at Fratta, left him by his brother-in-law Giorgio Loredan, a close friend who had been a fellow member in his youth of the Venetian Compagnia della Calza dei Cortesi. The change of ownership was between 1545 and 1548, but it was only in the mid-1550s that Badoer decided to provide a suitable residence on these estates.
The villa is declared as newly completed in a document dated August, 1556, when it was decided to rebuild the town bridge over the Scortico (the tributary of the Adige that flows past the house, separating it from the town), aligning it with the entrance to the new villa of the Badoer family. A map dated 1557 gives few details but shows the boundary walls, while the plan of the villa, with its hemicyclical outbuildings, is accurately recorded in a drawing from 1564 (both maps are published in AA.VV., 1984, pp. 37 and 40).
Work must have started no later than 1555; while the design would have followed Palladio's important journey to Rome in the company of Daniele Barbaro in 1554, when he extended his knowledge of the classical monuments. His examination of the building known as the "Villa of Maecenas" at Tivoli—the sketches he made are still extant—is mirrored in the two aedicules set near the orchard, which contrast with the old outer wall of the villa and its crenellations, reminiscent of the medieval castle of Salinguerra da Este (the brother-in-law of Ezzelino da Romano) which Palladio declares once stood on this site. Then the layout of the villa, with the residence set on a mound (partly because of fear of flooding) and the semicircle of porticoed outbuildings set lower down, is closely bound up with his interest in the curved walls he observed in ancient remains, such as the temple of Hercules Victor at Tivoli, or modern buildings like the Villa Madama. This is a feature that links the Villa Badoer with the Villa Thiene at Cicogna of almost the same date, and foreshadows the complex designs of the villas for the Trissino family at Meledo and Mocenigo "sopra la Brenta," published in the *Quattro Libri*.
The curving wings with their Tuscan columns masking the outhouses are not joined to the sides of the residence but stop in front of it—ending in a small pediment—at the point of attachment of the flights of steps at the sides, so allowing the villa to stand out with a monumental emphasis. At the same time the main flight of steps ascends with great deliberation up to the large portico of the *piano nobile*, screened by six slender Ionic columns supporting the slightly projecting pediment, which (in the architect's words) "makes a splendid sight, because it renders the central section taller than the sides." Judging by the design in the *Quattro Libri*, the hexastyle portico was meant to be repeated on the rear of the building, facing out over the countryside, projecting boldly from the façade. The entrance staircase is also very different in the design, being more complex, while the roof was lowered, allowing the pediment to stand out more emphatically in the completed building. The outbuildings stopped at the sixth intercolumn, and it was only at the end of the eighteenth century that they were extended to meet the boundary wall and a chapel set there. The layout of the rooms on the *piano nobile* corresponds to the design. They centre on the customary central axis, running through the great rectangular salon with its beamed roof, with the other rooms dovetailed

Drawing with plan and elevation of the Villa Badoer (from the "Quattro Libri").

into this pattern. The undercroft is among the most beautiful of all Palladio's designs, with the fascinating interplay of its vaults, displaying his consummate technical skill. Palladio tells us that the rooms of the *piano nobile* were decorated with "wonderfully imaginative grotesques by Giallo Fiorentino." They have only recently been brought to light again, through careful restoration which cleared away a thick layer of plaster, and are in fact extremely handsome, highly evocative in their refined symbolism, though the meaning is often obscure. The decoration as a whole seems to celebrate the reclamation of the land and the bonds of friendship between Francesco Badoer and Giorgio Loredan. So the jesters painted in the portico seem to allude to their youthful period of membership in the Compagnia della Calza; while the various divinities of river and wood, together with the pastoral scenes in the salon, can be taken as a tribute to the concept of agriculture as sacred, so dear to the owner of the villa. The themes of the side rooms are more private and melancholy. The large chamber contains depictions of *Leda and the Dioscuri* and the *Rape of Ganymede*, which seem to allude to the untimely death of Giorgio Loredan.

The ties of friendship and kinship uniting the

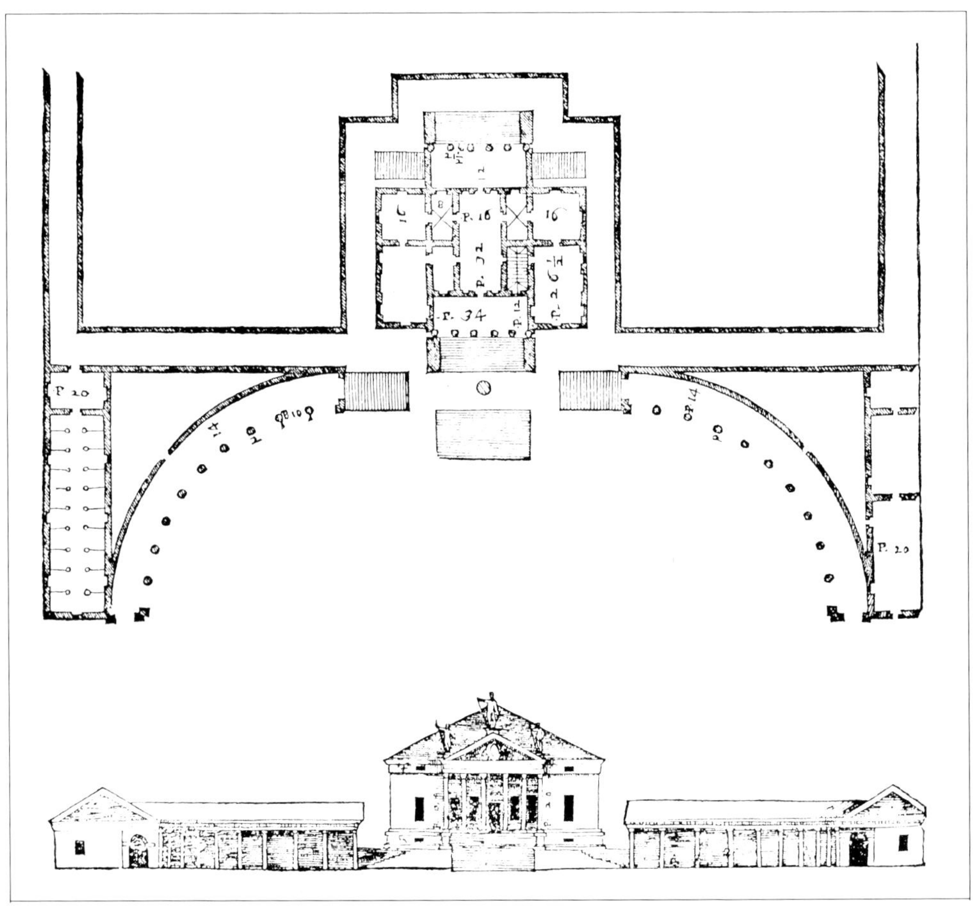

Villa Badoer, view of the whole and the central salon decorated with grotesques by Giallo Fiorentino.

two families are recorded in the fusion of their two family crests, a motif that recurs repeatedly in the decoration and originally also appeared on the pediment of the façade (then replaced by the arms of the Mocenigo family, the next owners of the villa).
Little is known of Giallo Fiorentino, called on to decorate the villa as soon as it was complete. Recent studies have found that his Christian name was Pierfrancesco, and that in 1553 he had assisted Giuseppe Porta, known as il Salviati, a Tuscan artist, to fresco the Loredans' Venetian palace at Santo Stefano. This refined and unusual artist is credited also with the decoration of the Villa Grimani-Molin, not far from the Villa Badoer, and what remains of the frescoes at the Villa Porto at Vivaro di Dueville. This is significant because both these buildings are attributed—though not certainly—to Palladio.

Bibliography: Vasari, 1568, p. 528; Palladio, 1570, l. II, p. 48; Muttoni, 1740, p. 21; Bertotti Scamozzi, 1781, pp. 43-45; Magrini, 1845, p. 240; Burger, 1909, pp. 110-112; Pane, 1961, p. 276; Crosato, 1962, p. 51; Guiotto, 1964, pp. 76 ff.; Wittkower, 1964, p. 74; Forssman, 1965, pp. 67 ff.; Ackerman, 1967, pp. 47-49; Zorzi, 1969, pp. 94-100; Puppi, 1972 and 1973, pp. 308-310; Cevese, 1973, pp. 74-77; Kubelik, 1974, pp. 446-447; Fairbairn, in Burns, 1975, pp. 237-238; Semenzato, 1975, pp. 45-49; Rigon, 1980, nos. 13-14; Tiozzo, 1981, pp. 37-41; Fontana, in AA.VV., 1984, pp. 36-37, 39-51; Rigobello, in AA.VV., 1984, pp. 52-54; Canova, 1985, pp. 152-163; Muraro, 1986, pp. 204-209; Bödefeld-Hinz, 1987, pp. 131-134; Costant, 1987, pp. 91-92; Rinaldi, 1989.

Villa Badoer, kitchen.

Villa Thiene

Cicogna di Villafranca Padovana (Padua), 1556; attribution certain, constructed in part.

Go as far as Grisignano di Zocco on the road between Vicenza and Padua, then take the road for Campodoro and Villafranca Padovana. On the far side of the village, towards Piazzola sul Brenta, an isolated group of farm buildings can be seen on the left; among them the outbuilding of Villa Thiene stands out clearly, with its right flank facing the road.

On page 62 of the second volume of the *Quattro Libri* Palladio presents a villa which he designed for the Thiene family. It was also referred to by Vasari in 1568. The building shown comprises a residence set on a high base, with two identical elevations, one facing the open countryside and the other the forecourt, with corner turrets suggestive of a castle at each end, not unlike those on the early Villa Muzani at Malo, Villa Pisani at Bagnolo or Villa Contarini at Piazzola. At the centre of each of the main façade there is a tall portico, comprising the two storeys of the building and screened by four Corinthian columns of a giant order supporting the pediment. Both the porticoes give access directly into a great square central hall, whose vaulting (Palladio himself tells us) rises up to the roof, while a series of Ionic columns set against the walls supports the gallery leading off into the suites upstairs. This scheme was used in numerous urban palaces and foreshadows the arrangement in the Rotonda, as well as the design for the Villa Trissino at Meledo. Two curved colonnades stretch out in front from the sides of the main steps "like arms emerging from the house," taking in the service buildings set opposite and along the sides of the courtyard. Only one of these outbuildings has come down to us, the other has been lost; while the main residence was never built.

The design for the villa was commissioned by Francesco Thiene, a nobleman of Vicenza, certainly by the end of 1556 (the year of his death), and was part of a much wider plan for reorganizing his estates at Cicogna, which had been going ahead since the 1540s, including the layout of a proper road network, which was also entrusted to the famous architect. The scheme met with a setback on Francesco's death, and was revived only in about 1563 by his sons, Teodoro and especially Odoardo, who seems to have been more closely connected with the renewal of the project at Cicogna. In that year we know work went on quickly, for a declaration made to the fiscal office in Padua by the brothers included a kiln for firing bricks for the new structures, namely the walls of the courtyard and the outhouse which has come down to us. The layout of the outhouse appears clearly in a map of 1564 (published by Kubelik, 1974, p. 452, and Puppi, 1974, p. 101), where it abuts onto a set of farm buildings laid out around two porticoed courtyards and comprising the old manor house. We know that the second outhouse was begun later on, but never finished, and that the foundations of the villa were also excavated, but the work must have ended here because the act of division of the estate between Teodoro's sons in 1597 shows that the situation was unchanged, as the neo-Palladian architect Francesco Muttoni found at the beginning of the eighteenth century.

The reason why the project came to nothing lies probably in the personal affairs of Odoardo Thiene. Since 1561 he had been connected with Calvinist circles in Vicenza and to escape the accusation of heresy he decided in 1567 to abandon the city for Geneva, leaving the work he had principally supported unfinished. The ideas of the reformers were widespread in Vicenza and many of Palladio's friends and clients—like the Godi, Repeta and Angarano families—sympathized with them, so that it has been thought that the architect himself may have been influenced by the movement. Besides, Palladio actually acted as a witness to the act of attorney by which Odoardo Thiene appointed his brother to look after his affairs on the eve of his secret flight to Switzerland.

The outbuilding which has survived has a portico with five arches (instead of the four of the engraving in the *Quattro Libri*), with Tuscan pilasters supporting the cornice, which is faithfully reproduced in a drawing (London, R.I.B.A., XVII, 20), considered a working copy of the original designs, prepared in about 1563 by the supervisor of the construction work. Evaluating the design

Drawing with plan and elevation of the Villa Thiene at Cicogna (from the "Quattro Libri").

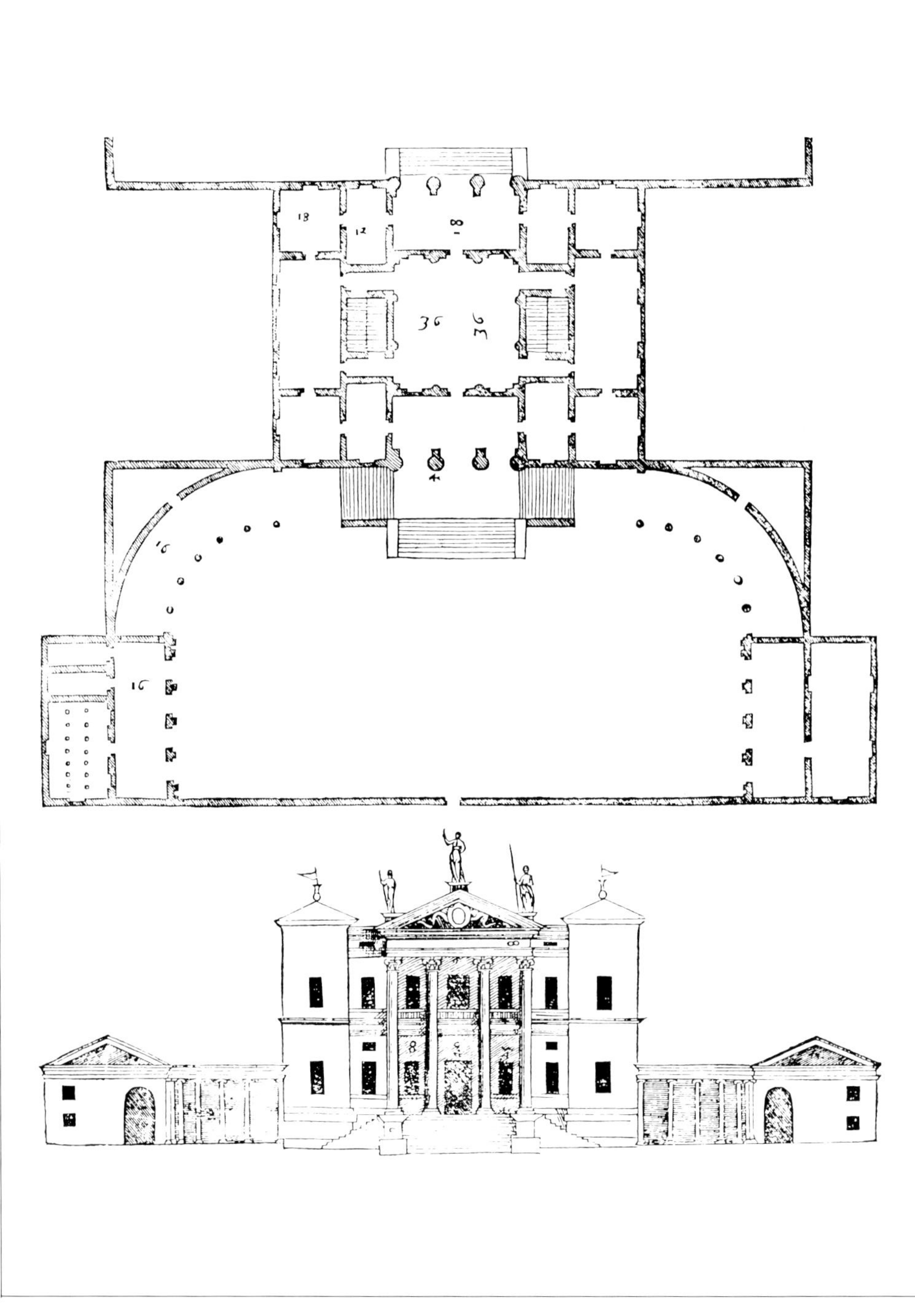

Villa Thiene (Cicogna), front view of the outbuilding.

published in the treatise is a complicated matter because while some elements (like the circular course of the porticoes and the way they join up with the staircase) correspond typologically to the design of the Villa Badoer or Villa Ragona, from about 1555, others (like the central chamber and the design of the façade) seem to belong to a later period. In other words some scholars think that the original design from 1556 was partially revised when work began again in 1563, or else for publication in the *Quattro Libri*.

Bibliography: Vasari, 1568, p. 528; Palladio, 1570, I.II, p. 62 and I.III, p. 7; Muttoni, 1740, p. 36; Bertotti Scamozzi, 1781, pp. 20-22; Magrini, 1845, pp. 238-241; Burger, 1909, pp. 37-40; Pane, 1961, pp. 275-276; Ackerman, 1967, p. 75; Zorzi, 1969, pp. 101-106; Puppi, 1973, pp. 311-313 and 1974, p. 101; Kubelik, 1974, p. 452; Costant, 1987, p. 88.

Villa Repeta

100 Campiglia dei Berici (Vicenza), 1557-1558 (?); attribution certain, destroyed.

From Vicenza follow the Riviera Berica towards Noventa Vicentina and turn right after Ponte di Barbarano, then continue as far as the centre of Campiglia dei Berici. The villa used to stand on the site of the present seventeenth century Villa Repeta.

Virtually nothing remains of the villa designed by Palladio for Mario Repeta, a nobleman of Vicenza. It was irremediably damaged by a fire in the later seventeenth century and perhaps the only surviving traces of it are the four Doric columns of the pronaos facing the countryside of the present building, promptly constructed to replace the earlier one in 1672, as shown by the inscription on the façade.

The loss of the villa is much to be regretted; one need only glance at the design in the *Quattro Libri* and read the description of it by Palladio to realize the exceptional qualities of the structure. Its conception must belong to after 1556, the year of Francesco Repeta's death, as we know from Palladio that his son Mario decided to build a new and more fitting home at Campiglia, to replace an old manor house, out of respect for his father's wishes. The exact date is uncertain (perhaps 1557-1558) but the villa was certainly being built in 1566, during Giorgio Vasari's last sojourn in the Veneto, as shown by his description of the building two years later in his *Lives*.

Here the customary distinction between a central, taller residence and the wings of outhouses is no longer maintained. Everything is developed on a single plane, and the various elements are arranged around the three sides of a great rectangular court, all screened in the same way by a continuous portico of Doric columns. Only the centre of the main side is distinguished by a small pediment, which leads the eye out into the countryside and divides the spaces to be occupied by the owners from the farm structures, while two dovecotes with double loggias on the outer side stand at the corners.

Palladio also tells us that the owner used to invite many friends to Campiglia, where he enjoyed rights of an almost feudal nature, and that some of the rooms in the new building were reserved for his guests. Each of these rooms was dedicated to a certain virtue (continence, justice, etc.) and frescoed with appropriate subjects by Alessandro Maganza, called il Magagnò, a painter and poet of Vicenza, so that each guest could choose his chamber to suit the virtue he felt most inclined towards. Mario Repeta was in fact a somewhat singular character. Probably connected with the Reforming circles in Vicenza, notably the Anabaptists, he held numerous gatherings in his house at Campiglia, and they were certainly not confined, as he wanted people to think, to humanist discussions about Petrarch. He was the object of an inquiry by the Holy Office in 1572. We also find him attacking openly the concept of authority and "the many injustices in governing and administering public affairs," so that some scholars see the unusually uniform structure of the villa as the embodiment of the owner's ideals, his dislike of the divisions between social classes, and aristocratic privilege.

Bibliography: Vasari, 1568, p. 258; Palladio, 1570, 1. II, . 61; Muttoni, 1740, pp. 35 ff.; Bertotti Scamozzi, 1781, pp. 16-17; Magrini, 1845, pp. 75, LXXII, 241, 330; Burger, 1909, pp. 83-86; Pane, 1961, p. 230; Ackerman, 1967, pp. 74-75; Tafuri, 1969, p. 132; Zorzi, 1969, pp. 119-124; Puppi, 1973, pp. 318-320; Kubelik, 1974, pp. 460-461; Muraro, 1978, 1981-1982 and 1986, p. 270.

Drawing of the plan and elevation of the Villa Repeta (from the "Quattro Libri").

Villa Repeta, elevation of the seventeenth century villa.

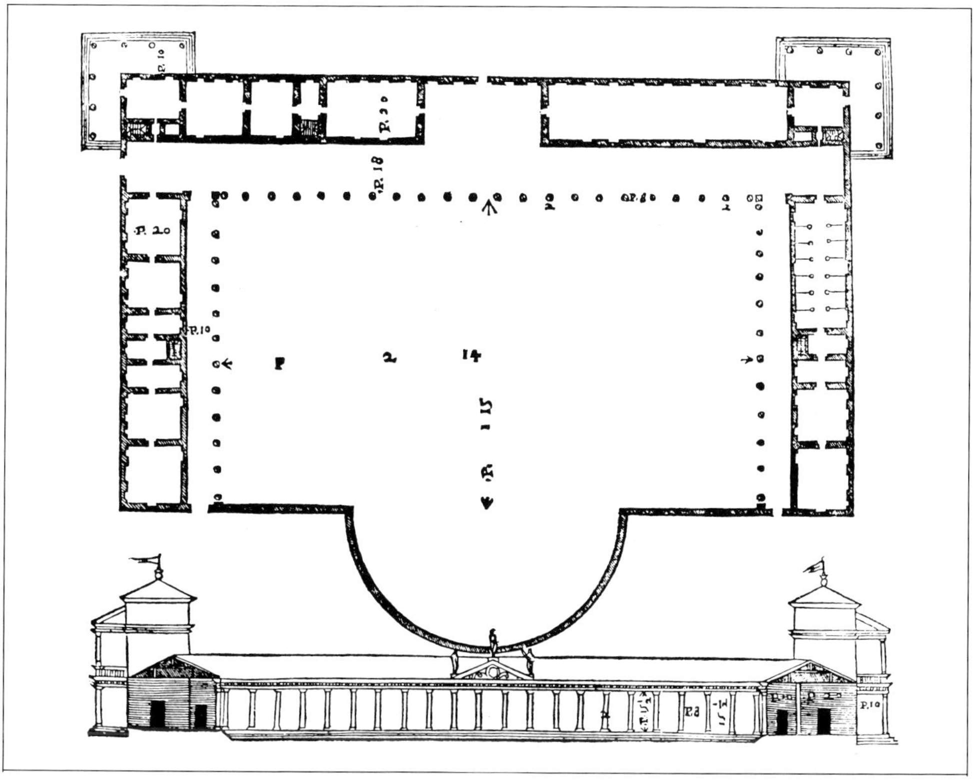

Villa Grimani Molin

102 Fratta Polesine (Rovigo),
1558-1559; attribution not certain.

The villa stands a few hundred metres to the left of the Villa Badoer (see the relevant entry).

The attribution of this villa to Palladio was suggested as early as the last century, but it has only recently been seriously investigated and is still much debated. Since these researches have shown that the villa belongs to the same period and cultural circles as the nearby Villa Badoer, it is worth looking more fully at the question, with the necessary reservations.
The villa stands about a hundred metres from the most celebrated building by Palladio, towards which it faces. It consists of a cube-shaped main residence with a pronaos emerging from its façade, screened by six Doric columns, set above a tall rusticated portico with five arches borne on pillars. As in the Villa Foscari at Malcontenta, which it resembles most closely in type, the pediment of the pronaos does not rise above the eaves of the roof. Access is provided by a double flight of steps at the sides. The windows of the *piano nobile* have a simple trabeated cornice while those on the ground floor and the smaller ones of the attic are sharp-edged.
The interior is laid out on a scheme recurrent in Palladio's buildings: the rooms are arranged symmetrically on either side of a large central chamber. Two outbuildings used to bound the sides of the forecourt, detached from the residential block; only the one on the right still exists. It is a two-storey edifice with five arches characterized by large keystones and framed by Tuscan pilasters.
The villa was built between 1557 and 1564 by Vincenzo Grimani, on land formerly belonging (as at the Villa Badoer) to Giorgio Loredan. On his death in 1538 part of the estate passed to his sister Lucetta, the wife of his close friend Francesco Badoer, and to Lucrezia, betrothed from the age of three to Vincenzo Grimani, who had been brought up like a son by the Badoer family and married her in 1541. The decision to build the new villa must have followed closely on that of their friend and brother-in-law. A map dated 1557 (published in AA.VV., 1984, p. 40), when the Villa Badoer had just been finished, shows a sizeable building on the site chosen. This must have been the earlier family mansion, which seems to have faced onto the Scortico canal, traversed by a bridge close by. Another map of 1564 (published in AA.VV., 1984, p. 37) shows clearly a newly completed villa, giving its ground plan with the two outbuildings at its sides.
Despite the uncertainties evident in its composition and the fact that it is not a very successful work (its weak points being the disproportion between the rectangular residential block and the pronaos, and the failure to link the outbuildings to the centre), no other architect save Palladio seems to have been capable in the late 1550s of conceiving such a striking spatial and typological design. If the attribution is accepted, then it can be conjectured that he did not supervise that construction; and there is in fact some slight evidence that Domenico Groppi (who collaborated elsewhere with the architect and claimed payments outstanding at Polisine in his will) was responsible for carrying out work without particular fidelity to the drawings.
It is noteworthy that the orientation of the new building completely ignores the watercourse and instead faces the Villa Badoer, which had become an important point of reference for the villa at Fratta.
There are further links between the two buildings. In 1564 the eldest daughter of Grimani, Isabetta, married Andrea Molin whose heirs later inherited the building. Giallo Fiorentino was called in on that occasion to celebrate the event with a fitting set of decorations. We have met the painter before, a few years earlier, in the neighbouring villa, which he had frescoed. Even more clearly than before, he revealed his gifts as an outstanding and refined painter of grotesques; while he was less skilled in the figurative scenes, due to his inability to render spatial depth. The dominant qualities of the whole cycle—confined to the salon and the suites on the left in the *piano nobile*—are the exaltation of beauty and female virtue. The walls of the great central chamber are divided into large panels by grotesques, framing the allegories of the Virtues, represented in the guise of ladies riding upon animals, so repeating identical themes in the Villa Badoer. In

Villa Grimani Molin, view of the whole.

the centre of the longer sides there are two great scenes with female figures. In the first room on the left there is a painting of Jove and Juno against an expanse of sky in the ceiling; below, certain members of the Grimani-Molin family lean out over a *trompe l'oeil* parapet. The next room is devoted to the Happy Spouses, who are depicted on the ceiling, surrounded by white doves. The walls present us with male figures of divinities. The last room shows a reclining woman (perhaps Cleopatra) represented in sequence the various stages of love, ending with the final sacrifice.

The frescoes, like the villa, have recently been carefully restored.

Bibliography: Canova, 1971, pp. 47-51; Semenzato, 1975, pp. 51-57; Tiozzo, 1981, pp. 19-22, 45-46; Castegnaro Barbuiani, in AA.VV., 1984, pp. 63-67; Puppi, in AA.VV., 1984, p. 10.

Villa Foscari, known as “La Malcontenta”

104 Gambarare di Mira, in the locality called Malcontenta (Venice),
1558-1559 (?); attribution certain.

The best way to reach the villa is to take a boat up the Brenta canal. By land, follow the Riviera del Brenta, which runs from Padua to Venice; at the crossroad after Oriago take the road for Malcontenta-Fusina. Another route runs directly from Mestre-Marghera in the direction of Fusina. The villa can be visited on Tuesday, Saturday and the first Sunday of each month from May to October, between 9 a.m. and 12 a.m., or on other days for groups of over ten by telephone booking (tel. 041/5470012).

The villa stands by a bend in the navigable Brenta canal, in a locality where, according to tradition, a noblewoman of the Foscari family was sent to live in solitude and make amends for her dissolute life. Hence the name “La Malcontenta” given first to the place and then the Palladian villa. If you come by water from Venice, the house can be glimpsed among the foliage of flourishing trees, but when it was built no vegetation screened it and one can imagine the impressive sight it made when it appeared quite unexpectedly, with its imposing classical pronaos, reminiscent of ancient Rome, so close to Venice with its stunning, flamboyant Gothic palaces.
It is not precisely known when the villa was designed. It had definitely been built by 1560, the year of the death of Nicolò Foscari, the moving spirit behind the project, as we know from a statement to the Venetian tax authorities made in 1566 by his brother Alvise, co-owner of the property. So its conception can be set at about 1558-1559, following the designs for the Villas Ragona and Badoer which resemble it by being set on a very high base. There are also similarities with the Villa Chiericati and Villa Cornaro, which both have a pronaos which is set well forward, and Villa Barbaro at Maser with the design of its cruciform chamber.
The building Palladio designed for the Foscari was created above all to project an image: a true suburban villa, freed from the administration of country estates and so without the need for outbuildings. Only later—presumably in the seventeenth century—was a service complex set next to it; this appears in eighteenth century engravings but no longer exists. As in other houses built close to a watercourse and so in danger of occasional flooding, the *piano nobile* is set on a tall plinth, together with the hexastyle pronaos with its Ionic columns. Access to this is provided not by the usual frontal staircase but by two flights of steps that wind up to it on either side, so that it looks like a “quotation” from the temple of Clitumnus, though there are also suggestions of the celebrated Pantheon in Rome. Then the pediment does not rise above the roof but dovetails into the façade below the line of the eaves and is repeated in the triangular outline of the attic above. The stately classicism of the north elevation contrasts with the patent functionality of the elevation facing onto the countryside, which meets the need to provide abundant light for the spaces inside, whose layout can be read clearly in its design. The projecting middle section corresponds to the great cruciform salon and is studded with apertures that centre on a thermal window; this indicates the barrel vaulting within the building and breaks up the base of the purely decorative pediment, traced by the cornices on the wall rather as if it were a projection of the one over the pronaos on the front. A triangular attic also rises above the roof on this side, flanked by two tall traditional chimneys.
All the outside walls are patterned by the dressed stonework, which also frames the windows, and recent restoration has re-established the interplay between the white stone of the walls and the *cotto* of the columns and other architectural features. The cruciform salon on the *piano nobile* is much larger than the one at Maser and revives memories of the interiors of the baths of ancient Rome. The light streams in from the southern façade, with its many windows looking out over the countryside, while seen from the inside the wall opposite faces onto the loggia of the pronaos towards the canal. Around this chamber, which is a prelude to the centralized salon of La Rotonda, the other rooms are laid out, of various different forms and divided by the arms of the cross.
The whole of the *piano nobile* is decorated with frescoes; unfortunately they are badly

Drawing of the plan and elevation of the Villa Foscari (from the "Quattro Libri").

damaged and many parts were torn off in the nineteenth century. Restoration work in 1976-1978 repaired some of the tears and the frescoes can now be viewed with pleasure.

The cycle deals with the usual themes of the Cinquecento villa, but the way the subjects are handled has many affinities with the decoration of the former castle of Francis I, King of France, at Fontainebleau, an important centre of Mannerist art. This supports the theory that the idea for the cycle came from Vittore Grimani, a friend of Foscari, who had lived for some years at the French court and was also responsible for part of the cycle of paintings in the Libreria Marciana in Venice, to which these frescoes show evident similarities.

Palladio states in his treatise that the decoration of the whole villa was the work of Giambattista Zelotti, except for part of a room begun by Battista Franco but broken off by his death in 1561. This fact allows us to fix a rough date for the whole cycle around this year. Franco is known as an artist trained in Rome who produced some drawings after Michelangelo; while for the Foscari he had earlier painted an altarpiece for the family chapel in the church of San Giobbe in Venice. The room he painted has been identified as the second to the left of the salon. It shows the fall of the Giants, who tumble down under the weight of enormous boulders, between ruined columns, while Jove (in the vault), surrounded by the gods of Olympus, strikes them with his thunderbolts. Franco seems responsible for the frescoes on the walls and Zelotti for those in the vault; but not all the scholars accept these attributions, while some even reverse the attributions.

All the rest of the decoration is by Zelotti,

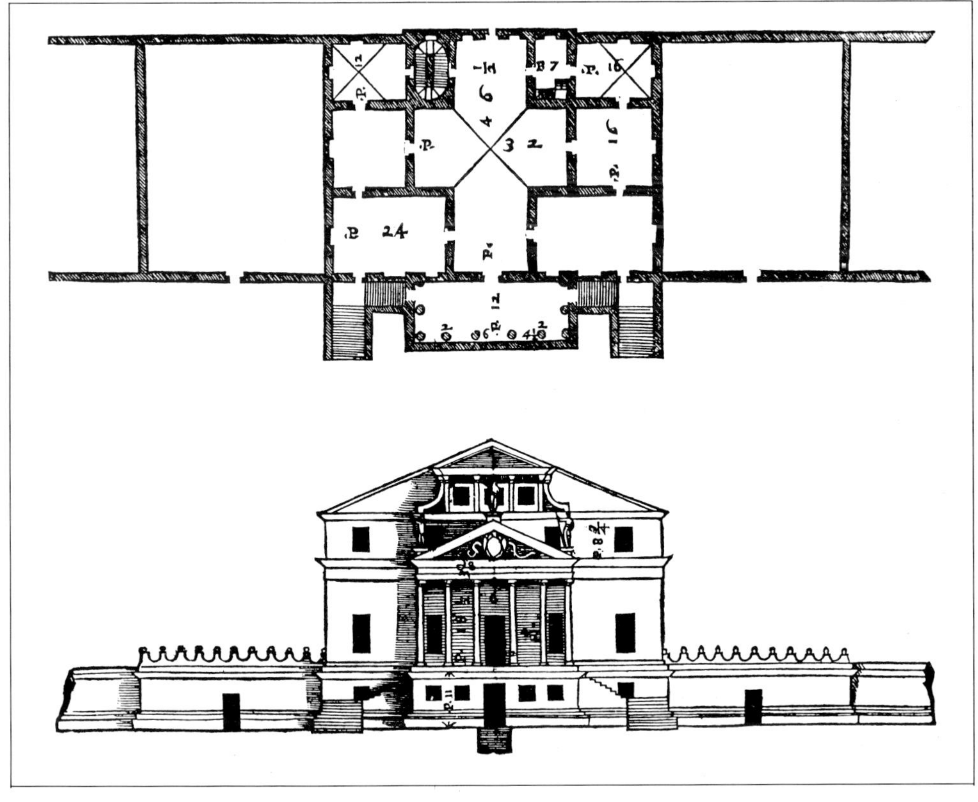

Villa Foscari, view of the whole from the canal and front elevation.

who had just completed the frescoes in the Villa Godi at Lonedo in about 1560. The painter divided up the walls of the salon with illusionistic Ionic columns, between which he set bronzed statues in niches, trophies, standards and, above the doorways, buxom female figures representing Astrology, Mathematics, Poetry and Bellona, the goddess of war. The lunettes that conclude the arms of the cross contain episodes from mythology—save the southern one, which is taken up by the thermal window—as do the ovals in the four barrel vaults, while the central hexagon presents the Virtues. Festoons, tablets, cupids and powerful male nudes fill the empty spaces in this ornamental composition, which is one of the most harmonious of Zelotti's works. The first room on the left is thronged with mythological subjects and architectural patterns. This room leads into the Chamber of the Giants, decorated with painted arcades framing the stories of Phaethon and Cacus, while a beautiful female figure, Juno or Abundance, is set over the mantelpiece. In the ceiling, above a frieze of cupids, women and marble busts, there is a medallion of Prometheus stealing fire from Jove. The room opposite, to the right of the entrance, possesses the largest intact frescoed surface. In the ceiling a beautiful Aurora sprinkles flowers from her flying chariot, while the painted arcades on the walls frame mythological scenes and we glimpse a woman entering through a doorway, a figure traditionally identified with "La Malcontenta" of the legend.

The decoration of the middle room on the right is badly damaged. It is devoted to Bacchus and Cupid. By great good fortune part of the frescoes lost were found detached and rolled up in a fabric in a nearby barn and recuperated. The Museum of Castelvecchio in Verona contains the first section torn from the south wall, depicting Venus enflaming hearts with the aid of Cupid and Music. On the opposite side, beyond a painted balustrade, there is a Sacrifice to Bacchus; above it a pergola interwoven with vine stems opens to the sky, revealing the god of wine crushing a bunch of grapes into a chalice held by Cupid, with Venus nearby. The frescoes in the two southern chambers at the sides of the salon are stunning in their elegance and beauty:

Villa Foscari, room decorated with grotesques and cruciform salon, both frescoed by Giambattista Zelotti.

Villa Foscari, the Fall of the Giants, detail, fresco attributed to Battista Franco.

they represent grotesques, alternating with landscapes. Their ceilings are decorated with medallions containing the figures of Fame (on the left) and Time (on the right).

Bibliography: Vasari, 1568, p. 528; Palladio 1570, 1.II, p. 50; Muttoni, 1740, pp. 22-23; Bertotti Scamozzi, 1781, pp. 9-11; Magrini, 1845, pp. 76, LXXII, 330; Burger, 1909, pp. 88-93; Pane, 1961, pp. 228 ff.; Crosato, 1962, pp. 136-140; Guiotto, 1964, pp. 74-76; Wittkower, 1964, pp. 125-126; Forssman, 1965, pp. 61 ff.; Ackerman, 1967, pp. 53-56; Pallucchini, 1968, pp. 212-213; Zorzi, 1969, pp. 151-156; Cevese, 1973, pp. 73-74; Forssman, 1973; Puppi, 1973, pp. 328-330; Tiozzo, 1977, pp. 57-60; Crosato Larcher, 1978; Foscari, 1978; Goedicke-Slusallek-Kubelik, 1980, pp. 97-100; Guiotto, 1980; Rigon, 1980, nos. 19-21; Tiozzo, 1981, pp. 25-34; Canova, 1985, pp. 186-197; Muraro, 1986, pp. 258-267; Bassi, 1987, pp. 63-83; Bödefeld-Hinz, 1987, pp. 138-140; Costant, 1987, pp. 95-96.

Villa Mocenigo

Drawing with plan and elevation of the Villa Mocenigo at Marocco (from the "Quattro Libri").

Marocco di Mogliano Veneto (Treviso), 1561-1562; attribution certain, partially constructed then destroyed.

The villa used to stand at Marocco, on the road from Mestre to Treviso, near the bridge over the Dese.

The building erected for the "clarissimo cavalier il signor Leonardo Mocenigo in a town called Marocco which lies on the road from Venice to Treviso" is one of the group of Palladian villas that has been lost, having been destroyed in the early nineteenth century. Leonardo Mocenigo, of a noble Venetian family, was on close and respectful terms with Palladio; their relationship had begun in the early 1550s when he had commissioned a villa for a site "on the Brenta," followed by other important works (see the relevant entries). For his estate in Marocco—if we can judge by the illustration in the *Quattro Libri*—Palladio had designed a structure that derives from the Villa Pisani at Montagnana, characterized by a double loggia (here hexastyle) surmounted by a pediment, which opens out in the centre of the façade, and by a ground plan centred on a chamber with four columns which is set at the back of the house and divided from the loggia by the paired free-standing staircases which "rise opposite one another, so that one can ascend and descend on the

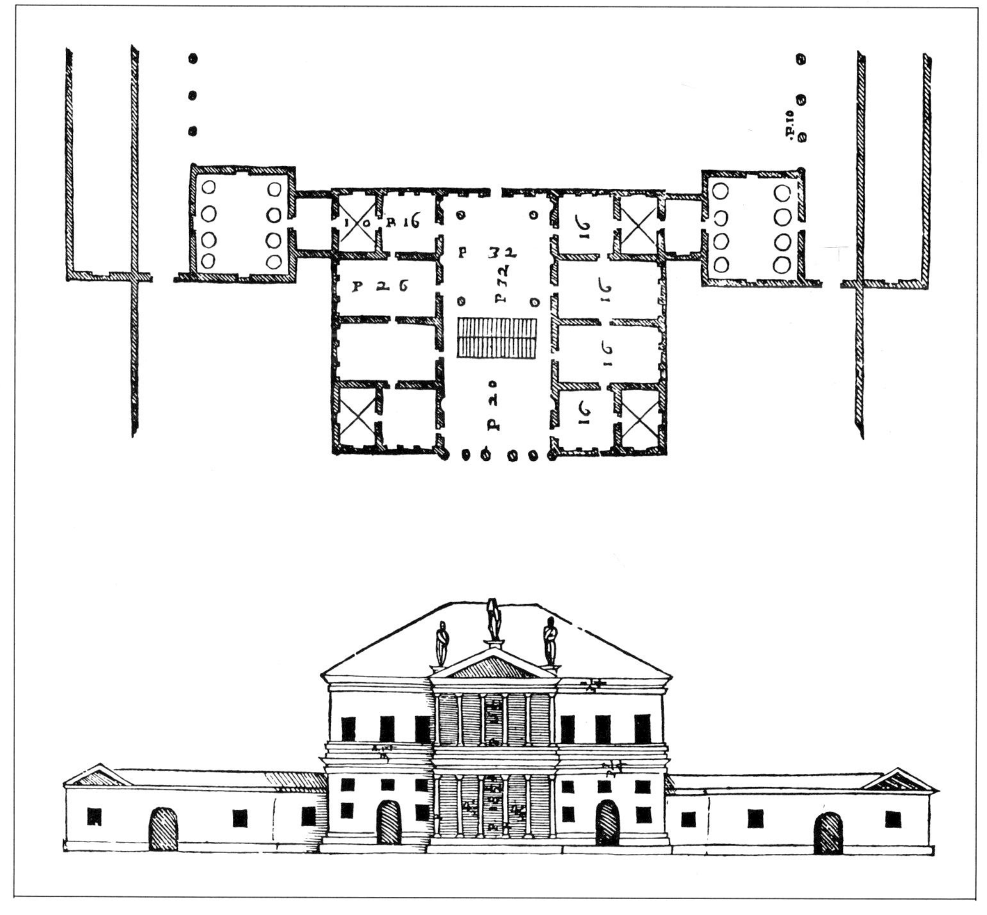

right or on the left and they are very convenient and beautiful." In keeping with this kin of suburban villa or villa-palace, the service buildings do not enclose the residential block but, though they stretch out from its sides, are relegated to a rear court.
It is not certain when the villa was designed and built. Probably in 1561-1562, the terms within which we can date two autograph drawings by Palladio that show sketches of the groundplan of the new building. They can be found together with two other drawings by Cristoforo Sorte, a sixteenth century cartographer, in a volume of documents which belonged to him (published in Burns, 1975, pp. 222-223); they are thought to have served to locate the exact position of the new building, in view of a request to change the course of some waterway to favour Mocenigo's estate, and would therefore have been executed for submission to the relevant Venetian magistrature. Since the sketches contain certain small variations in layout it seems reasonable to suppose that the design had not yet been fixed or the foundations laid. At any rate work seems to have been concluded as early as 1562, as shown by an inscription noted on the site by the nineteenth century scholar Antonio Magrini. But despite Vasari's statement in the *Lives* of 1568 that seems to imply that the villa had been built in full (he may have been deducing this from the architect's notes rather than direct observation), all that was completed of the entire program was the third section on the right (facing south), which got no further than the lower loggia and a small segment of the columns above. Besides, as both Francesco Muttoni and Ottavio Bertotti Scamozzi noted in the eighteenth century, the great staircase had been placed off-centre, the rooms were different in their proportions, the roofing was different and a fourth storey had been added to the edifice.

Bibliography: Vasari, 1568, p. 528; Palladio, 1570, 1.II, p. 54; Muttoni, 1740, p. 26; Bertotti Scamozzi, 1781, pp. 38-40; Magrini, 1845, p. 241; Burger, 1909, pp. 118-120; Pane, 1961, p. 221; Ackerman, 1967, pp. 76-77; Zorzi, 1969, pp. 186-187; Puppi, 1973, pp. 330-331; Burns, 1975, pp. 222-223; Lewis, 1981, p. 100; Puppi, 1987, pp. 339-340.

Villa Sarego

Drawing with plan and elevation of the Villa Sarego at Miega (from the "Quattro Libri").

Miega di Veronella (Verona),
1562; attribution certain, partially built and then destroyed.

Take the state highway from Vicenza to Verona, then turn left at Alte Ceccato and take the road towards Legnago; at Caselle turn right for Albaredo. Miega is the first village on this stretch of road and the courtyard with surviving outbuildings of the Villa Sarego can be seen from the road on the left, behind the church.

In 1562 *conte* Annibale Sarego of Verona decided to build a new country house on the estates at Miega, which he had inherited in 1552, and commissioned the most famous architect of the day, Andrea Palladio. It is worth pointing out that Palladio had already designed a palace in Verona for Sarego's brother-in-law, Giambattista Della Torre, and he was later commissioned by his brother Marcantonio to design the highly ambitious complex of Santa Sofia in Valpolicella and his cousins Antonio and Federico for villas at Cucca and perhaps also at Veronella and Beccacivetta.
The designs for the villa at Miega—subsequently published in the *Quattro Libri*—were delivered before 11 July 1562, the day when Palladio, returning from Brescia where he had worked as a consultant on the town hall, received payment of two gold *scudi* from Annibale Sarego. The sum is recorded in a valuable ledger kept by Sarego's steward, who also registered all the expenses of construction. From this we know that work only began in July 1564 with the digging of the foundations and continued rapidly all through the following year. There are records of further payments for work on the villa in 1566, after which construction was most likely suspended, leaving the building unfinished.
The illustration published in the *Quattro Libri* suggests that Palladio here repeated the well-tried model of the villa-palace, which he had first produced for the Pisani family at Montagnana, with a double order of loggias in the centre of the façade, supporting the pediment. A valuation of the property in 1678 shows, however, that only the right-hand side (comprising four rooms on each floor and part of the lower loggia) had been completed, while the outbuildings—which Palladio describes for us, though they are not in the illustration—were reorganized and extended in 1673. In the eighteenth century Francesco Muttoni noted that only the columns remained of the loggia, and Bertotti Scamozzi found that the original location of the inside staircase had not been respected, at the same time complaining of the ugliness of the surviving Corinthian capitals. The remains of the villa were finally destroyed shortly after 1910 and another villa built on the foundations. All that remains of Palladio's work is a single Ionic capital; while the long ranges of arched outbuildings remodelled in the seventeenth century also present some affinities with those of the other villas Palladio built for the Sarego family at what used to be called Cucca (now known as Veronella).

Bibliography: Palladio, 1570, 1.II, p. 68; Muttoni, 1740, p. 45; Bertotti Scamozzi, 1781, pp. 14-15; Magrini, 1845, p. 241; Biadego, 1886, pp. 15-19; Burger, 1909, pp. 93-95; Pane, 1961, p. 223; Ackerman, 1967, p. 78; Zorzi, 1969, pp. 187-192; Puppi, 1973, p. 348; Marini, in AA.VV., 1980 (IV), pp. 244-246.

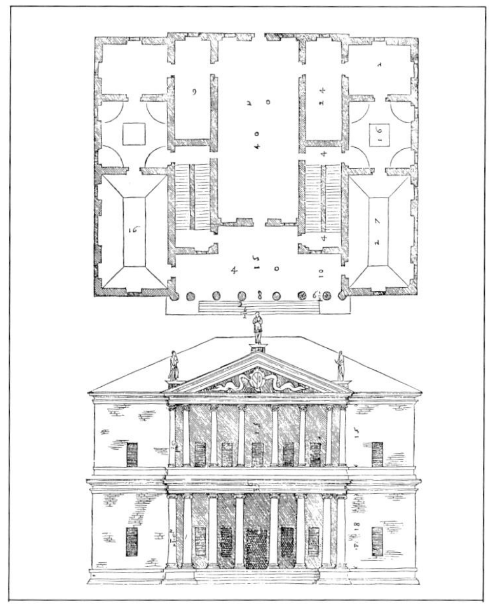

Villa Valmarana

Drawing with the plan and elevation of the Villa Valmarana at Lisiera (from the "Quattro Libri").

Lisiera di Bolzano Vicentino (Vicenza), c. 1563; attribution certain, constructed in part, half-destroyed then reconstructed.

The villa, with its fifteenth century outbuildings, is located in the centre of Lisiera, on state highway no. 53 that goes from Vicenza to Treviso, on the left.

The villa was commissioned (Palladio tells us in the *Quattro Libri*) by Gianfrancesco Valmarana, a nobleman active in the public administration of Vicenza and the brother of Giovanni Alvise. (Alvise's widow, Isabella Nogarola, was later to commission Palladio in 1565 to design the splendid palace on Corso Fogazzaro in Vicenza in memory of her husband.) As Valmarana died early in October 1566, the design must have been conceived before then; this is confirmed by Vasari, who saw the drawings for the villa during his travels in the Veneto in 1566. The date cannot be set much earlier, either, because of its evident affinities with the villa designed for the Thiene family at Cicogna, which seems to have been designed in about 1563 and was left unfinished because of its owner's death.
The Lisiera estates had long been in the Valmarana family and they exercised almost feudal rights over them, as well as control of the waterways and the right to exact a tax from people crossing the bridges. The site chosen for the new villa was already occupied by a Quattrocento manor house and outbuildings, of which all we have left is a farm building with dovecote towers. Palladio had to retain part of this complex of existing buildings, which he seems to have considered still functional; he declares that he left the rear courtyard unaltered, "with all the places related to the uses of the villa." He re-used at least part of an older edifice for the main residence, and this might explain the rather awkward layout apparent in the design published in the *Quattro Libri* and the presence of the four corner turrets, which seem to belong to a structure like the complex that Palladio had converted for Giangiorgio Trissino at Cricoli. Here he proposed to link the turrets by slender stairwells, stepped back slightly, to the front and back façades–the latter facing onto the courtyard. Each elevation had a broad double loggia with six columns and a pediment rising above the level of the whole building. But this scheme was never completed.
On the death of Valmarana work was suspended with only the first order of the front loggia complete; and many decades were to pass before his heirs decided to complete it as best they could. Work was carried out, perhaps in the early years of the next century, when the delightful family chapel adjoining it was erected (1615), resulting in the present incongruous and misproportioned building, quite different from the designs published in the treatise in 1570. The rear elevation was deprived of the loggia and lateral features (the turrets and stairwells) and the first order of the front loggia was surmounted by a low-ceilinged storey, a kind of attic with five rectangular windows and a balustrade set back, seventeenth century in style. Above this there is an excessively large pediment, while the turret no longer projects above the house because it has been annulled by the uniformly level roof. In addition to all this the

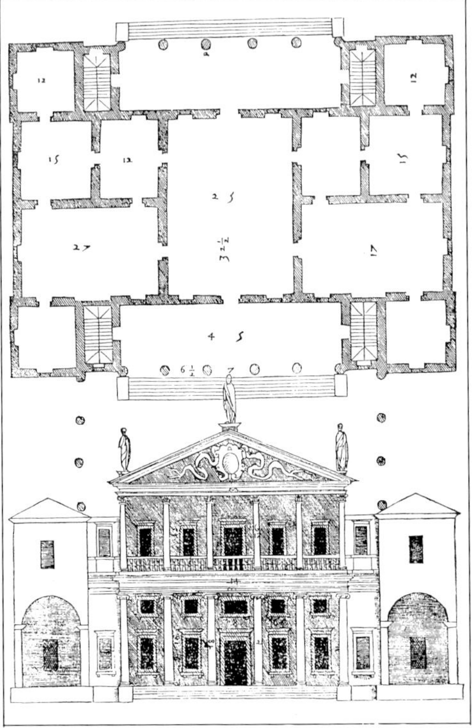

Villa Valmarana (Lisiera), front elevation of the present building.

building suffered extensive bomb damage in the last war. The front garden was rearranged in the early eighteenth century by the sculptor Francesco Marinali the Younger; together with assistants from his workshop he executed the numerous statues populating it. The statues crowning the façade of the villa are seventeenth century work.

Bibliography: Vassari, 1568, p. 528; Palladio, 1570, 1.II, p. 59; Muttoni, 1740, pp. 32-33; Bertotti Scamozzi, 1778, pp. 29-32; Magrini, 1845, p. 212; Burger, 1909, pp. 32-36; Pane, 1961, pp. 233 ff.; Ackerman, 1967, pp. 49-50; Zorzi, 1969, pp. 198-201; Cevese, 1971, II, p. 341; Puppi, 1973, pp. 350-351 and 1974, p. 101; Kubelik, 1974, pp. 459-460; Canova, 1985, pp. 202-204; Costant, 1987, pp. 111-112.

Villa Emo

114 Fanzolo di Vedelago (Treviso), 1564; attribution certain.

Starting from Castelfranco Veneto, take the state highway for Treviso, but turn left at Vedelago for Fanzolo; the villa is easily identified in the centre of Fanzolo. It can be visited on Saturday, Sunday and other public holidays (closed from Christmas Day to Epiphany). From May to September, open 3 p.m.-6 p.m.; from October to April, open 2 p.m.-5 p.m. For groups of over ten people it can be opened at other times by telephone booking (tel. 0423/487040).

Villa Emo is one of the very few works by Palladio that corresponds in every part (unimportant details aside) to the engravings of it published in the *Quattro Libri*. Its simplicity and the harmony of its proportions make it one of his finest works, fulfilling his ideal of a functional, practical building as well as embodying the equally important need to celebrate the culture and social rank of its owner, as was expected of a great country house.
The villa is laid out horizontally and spreads out into the surroundings with its long lines of outbuildings, each with eleven arches borne on simple pilasters. They contain—as Palladio points out—"the cellar space, barns, cattle sheds and other farm structures... and at the ends are two dovecotes that are of practical use to their master and of decorative effect to the building, and all these can be visited without going out into the open, which is one of the main points to be observed in a country house."
A broad flight of steps with a large flat space half-way up (not identical to the one in the *Quattro Libri* but definitely by Palladio) enhances the classical pronaos with its four Doric columns incorporated into the central section of the residence, and invites us into the penumbra of the portico. The columns project from the middle of the façade; those to the sides also round off the straight edges of the walls, graduating the transition from shadow to the brightness of the smooth outer surfaces, which are only broken up by the stringcourse of the plinth and the sharp edges of the windows.
The triangular pediment contains the crest of the Emo family supported by two fine Winged Victories which may well be the work of Alessandro Vittoria.
The interior is divided into three sections. An identical section on either side, each consisting of three rooms; and the central section that extends from the loggia, through a narrow vestibule, into the rear salon, where the view from windows faces out onto the flat, verdant countryside beyond. According to Palladio this enclosed orchard measured not less than eighty *campi* (the surface measure in use in the area), but we know that around the middle of the sixteenth century the Emos' estates at Fanzolo amounted to over four hundred *campi*. This shows just how important the outbuildings must have been in this villa. Leonardo Emo, the grandfather of Palladio's patron (also called Leonardo) had begun extensive reclamation work here in the early years of the century, on land purchased after the War of the League of Cambrai. He then set to work to farm it rationally by planting it with maize—then a new crop—perhaps under the influence of the patrician Alvise Cornaro of Padua, a sturdy promotor of the ideals of "sacred agriculture."
In a declaration to the Venetian tax authorities in 1537, Leonardo Emo senior lamented that he had a household of thirty-six people to support—in particular his son Giovanni with his eight children and the five orphans of his other son Alvise—and listed among his possessions an old farmhouse kept as a residence at Fanzolo, but so decrepit that it was urgently in need of reconstruction (Archivio di Stato di Venezia, Savi alle Decime, b. 97, c. 540). It is not clear whether he was able to set his hand to the work in the last two years of life left to him, or whether it was left to the heirs of the Fanzolo estates, his son Giovanni and the future patron of Palladio, Leonardo di Alvise, barely seven years old at the time (having been born in 1532). Be that as it may, Giovanni and his family lived in their own manor house at Fanzolo and included it regularly in their statements to the tax office in Castelfranco Veneto in 1546 and 1561 as a single property (Biblioteca Comunale di Castelfranco Veneto, Estimi antichi, b. 24, c. 511). It is not known when this building was replaced by the Palladian villa but it seems that here, too, the architect was working on an earlier structure, a hypothesis confirmed by the sim-

plicity of the tripartite plan.

The design of the new villa could hardly be earlier than 1553, when Leonardo came of age, or later than 1565-1566, the final date we can set for the drafting of the manuscript of the *Quattro Libri* containing the description of the building by Palladio's son Silla. (The manuscript is now in the Biblioteca Correr in Venice.) The scholars have suggested various dates between these extremes. Some have even proposed early 1539, claiming Leonardo senior commissioned the house; but this is hardly reasonable: if the property had not yet been divided between Giovanni and his nephew Leonardo Emo, it is highly unlikely that such extensive improvements would have been undertaken.

There is a general tendency to date the villa to about 1564, when the marriage of Leonardo to Cornelia Grimani had been fixed for the following year. In 1566 work was still going ahead, as we know from the fact that building workers were recorded as still on the site (Archivio di Stato di Vicenza, b. 548, c. 49), while the family chapel was completed in 1567, inserted in the outbuilding on the left (though it is not shown in the treatise). It is clear that a considerable building project had been carried out in the meantime from the valuation presented in 1573 by Leonardo Emo, in which he states that instead of the old manor house there was "a palace... with a boundary wall comprising sixty *campi*."

The splendid fresco cycle, in a perfect state of preservation, is generally dated to about 1565. They were the work of Giambattista Zelotti, as Palladio himself tells us, and cover the entire *piano nobile* of the villa. After the very fine earlier frescoes at the Villa Godi and Villa Malcontenta (to mention only two Palladian villas, though the artist was very busy with other commissions in the 1560s), Zelotti—the companion of Veronese in his early career—achieved a wholly personal expressive fullness here. Set within the customary framework of painted architectural features—which Palladio seems to have helped design, as at Lonedo—Zelotti painted episodes from mythology and Roman history, and allegories exalting the subjugation of the

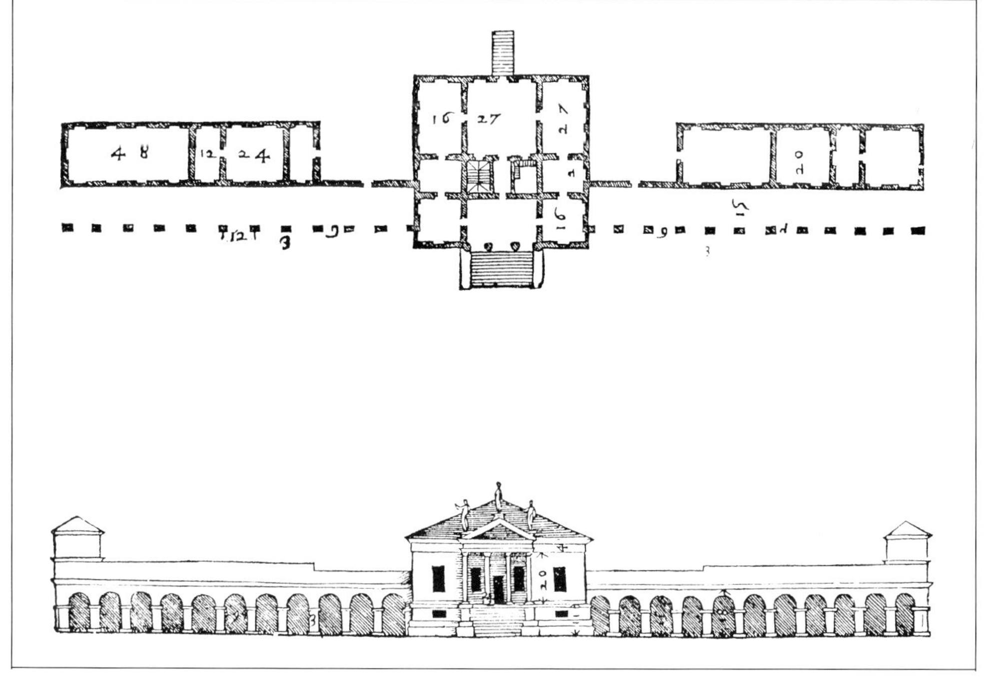

Drawing with the plan and elevation of the Villa Emo (from the "Quattro Libri").

Villa Emo, view of the front elevation and the front elevation of the residential section.

116

Villa Emo, The Death of Virginia, fresco by Giambattista Zelotti.

passions and the practice of the virtues which can only be achieved in the countryside, in peace, study and the devotion to agriculture. A celebration of the humanist ideals that guided the inhabitants of the villa, the home of all virtue.
At the sides of the loggia, divided by fluted Ionic columns and set above imitation doors, there are depictions of two mythical subjects with landscape settings: Callisto seduced by Jove and Callisto maltreated by Juno. Above the main doorway there is the figure of Ceres with ears of wheat in her hair and the tools of agriculture. In the vaulting of the ceiling there is a pergola of intertwined vines and on the walls monochrome allegorical figures of Cordiality and Thrift face each other above an imitation marble plinth which continues into the salon. Here the simplicity of this square chamber with its coffered ceiling is enhanced by the majestic Corinthian columns used to divide up the side walls into three sections. The two central spaces contain large paintings in praise of the virtue and chastity of the Ancients, with *The Continence of Scipio* and the *Death of Virginia*, while the sides have paintings of bronze statues, set within niches and symbolizing the four Elements, amid trophies, garlands, and powerful nude figures seated on the plinth. Over the main door there is a broken tympanum supporting the female figures of Prudence and Abundance.
The frescoes in the other rooms symbolize not only the liberal arts but also the human passions, through episodes from the lives of the pagan divinities; the way each is inserted within a panel of a religious character seems to suggest a didactic intention. The great chamber to the left, on the north side, is devoted to Hercules, depicted in two spacious panels, casting Lichas into the sea and embracing Deianeira. Over the mantelpiece we see Hercules burning in flames, rendered with rapid, intensely luminous touches of paint. The refined nude personifying Glory (above the door) is admirable. The figure of Christ appearing to Mary Magdalene (over the other door) is affected and sentimental. A delightful antechamber decorated with grotesques leads into the south room, devoted to the Arts, personified as beautiful life-sized maidens in splendid many-hued dresses, urging the viewer to cultivate astronomy, poetry, music, sculpture, painting and architecture. The Arts are set between ruined columns, while the monochrome depictions of Summer and Winter face each other from opposite walls. Above the door there is a Holy Family. The north room in the right wing is devoted to Venus, and has the same decorative layout as the chamber with Hercules. The goddess appears in the panels on the walls; she is shown trying to dissuade Adonis from the hunt and sustaining him when he has been wounded, while over the fireplace she is shown wounded by Cupid. The airy atmosphere of the mythical tales is set off against the dry and withered figure of St. Jerome penitent, above the door. Then follows another antechamber decorated with grotesques and finally the south chamber, decorated with stories framed by a colonnade and devoted to Io, the maiden loved by Jove and transformed into a heifer by the jealous Juno. The landscape settings are clear and the figures depicted with a preciosity unusual in Zelotti's work. Here, too, there is a marked contrast with the panel above the door, a vigorous Ecce Homo.

Bibliography: Palladio, 1570, l. II, p. 55; Muttoni, 1740, p. 27; Bertotti Scamozzi, 1781, pp. 23-25; Magrini, 1845, p. 240; Burger, 1909, pp. 102-104; Pane, 1961, pp. 227-228; Crosato, 1962, pp. 112-116; Wittkower, 1964, pp. 126-127; Ackerman, 1967, pp. 44-46; Pallucchini, 1968, pp. 214-216; Rupprecht, 1968, pp. 236-238; Zorzi, 1969, pp. 164-168; Bordignon Favero, 1970; Cevese, 1973, pp. 81-82; Puppi, 1973, pp. 352-353; Boucher, in Burns, 1975, p. 197; Bordignon Favero, 1978; Rigon, 1980, nos. 22-23; Canova, 1985, pp. 205-217; Muraro, 1986, pp. 240-255; Bödefeld-Hinz, 1987, pp. 148-149; Costant, 1987, pp. 103-104.

Villa Sarego at Cucca

Veronella (Verona),
1564 and 1569; attribution certain,
partially executed.

Take the state highway between Vicenza and Verona, turn left at Alte Ceccato, and drive through Cologna Veneta and so to Veronella, formerly known as Cucca. The villa complex which once belonged to the Sarego family lies behind the parish church and is surrounded by a battlemented wall. The outbuildings attributed to Palladio bound two consecutive sides of the forecourt.

On 23 August 1564 Federico Sarego paid 4 crowns to Andrea Palladio "for having revised the design of the building at Cucca." These words tell us of the existence of another project undertaken by Palladio in the Verona region; we know little about its precise nature, there is no mention of it in the *Quattro Libri*, and no more of it seems to have been built than the outhouses. These still exist, and comprise two long, low structures set at right angles to each other, with arches and semicolumns whose mouldings correspond to those of the surviving outbuildings at the nearby Villa Miega, designed by Palladio for Annibale Sarego, the cousin of Federico and brother of Marcantonio, who in the same years were beginning work on the important project for Santa Sofia in Valpolicella, also designed by Palladio.

The members of the family seem to have been driven by a spirit of emulation to develop their estates, providing suitable facilities for their administration and commissioning the architect best equipped to carry out such work. Federico, like his brother Antonio, owned extensive properties in the Verona region, but the Cucca estate was by far the oldest and most important. It also included a large residential complex, shown schematically in a map from c. 1565-1566 (see AA.VV., 1980, pp. 246-247). It comprised a defensive mediaeval structure which rose above two outhouses. The one set in front of the building seems to be the one that still exists, without the right wing set at 90 degrees to the outhouse. Records show that the outhouses were built between 1564 and 1567, so it is highly likely that the commission that earned Palladio 4 crowns was confined to designing the courtyard with all the facilities needed to run the estate; and it was only later that the family decided to redesign the old manor house. The frequent letters that passed between the brothers shows that in early October 1569 the architect was again called to Cucca and paid 2 *scudi* "to make a drawing of the palace and all the rest that we plan to build eventually." This clearly means that a survey of the existing building underlay the intention to restructure it.

The papers of the Sarego family reveal Palladio's unusual behaviour on this occasion. It seems that he was busy working on the draft of the *Quattro Libri* at the time, and so he failed to tackle this commission with his customary readiness. In the following November Federico wrote to him from Venice, urging him to deliver the drawings, so that the winter could be spent collecting the building materials. Then in December when he had received the plan of the building and, after much effort, the elevations, he declared himself dissatisfied and complained of being dealt with "alla nicolota," that is without due care and attention. And again in the following summer, when the architect's presence was urgently called for to oversee the start of work, Palladio kept his client waiting and lingered at Vicenza where he was building the palace in Via Porti for the nobleman Montano Barbarano. It was only on September 5 that he finally appeared at Cucca, to "consider the building that is to be constructed." Whether because Federico was dissatisfied with the design or financial problems cropped up, the project was never completed, and some years later Federico was considering renting out the estate. Only in the later eighteenth century was a villa partially constructed, near the mediaeval nucleus, and this is what can be seen on the site today.

Bibliography: Biadego, 1886, pp. 15-19; Ackerman, 1967, p. 78; Puppi, 1973, pp. 362-363; Viviani, 1975, pp. 797-799; Tavella-Castellazzi, in AA.VV., 1980 (IV), pp. 246- 247.

Villa Sarego

120 Veronella (Verona),
1564; design (?), never built.

The old town of Veronella lay a few kilometres from the present town of the same name (see previous entry), towards Verona.

Federico and Antonio Sarego may have commissioned Palladio to produce another design for a villa; the conjecture is based on a document dated 23 August 1564 notifying payment of 4 crowns to the architect "for revising the design of the building at Cucca and producing another plan for Veronella" (see the previous entry). The old locality of Veronella lies a few kilometres from the present town of that name (formerly called Cucca), on the road leading to Verona. The brothers also possessed estates here, and were gradually increasing their possessions. In 1559 they had bought a manor house with its outbuildings. The design supplied by Palladio in 1564 may have referred to the renewal of this structure or the provision of outbuildings, as at Cucca, but in fact we are unable to say whether work ever got under way at Veronella, as no record has come down to us and there is no structure there we can identify with a project by Palladio.

Bibliography: Biadego, 1886, pp. 15-19; Marini, in AA.VV., 1980 (IV), p. 252.

Villa Sarego

Santa Sofia di Pedemonte, in the commune of San Pietro in Cariano (Verona), 1565; attribution certain, partially constructed.

Take the state highway no. 12 from Verona towards Rovereto-Trento as far as Parona di Valpolicella. The main entrance to the villa is on the old road from this town to San Pietro in Cariano, near Pedemonte, in the locality named Santa Sofia.

Palladio tells us in the *Quattro Libri* that the villa built for the *conte* Marcantonio Sarego in Valpolicella is "placed on a fine site, at the top of a hill which can easily be ascended, that reveals part of the town and is set between two small valleys; all the hills around are delightful and abound in fresh water, so that this house is adorned with gardens and marvellous fountains." The building we see today corresponds to not even half of the design in the treatise, consisting of the left-hand side of the central courtyard. So that what we see as the façade is no more than the section of a porticoed peristyle. The U-shaped fragment is fascinating, to say the least, and quite unique in Palladio's work. A giant order of Ionic columns runs round the three inner sides, supporting an elegant trabeation with a frieze and floral volutes. The columns are unusual because their shafts are not smooth but made up of large, roughly worked stones, set one above the other, whose rustication absorbs the light in a way that is highly effective. In Palladio's own words, they "have behind them, below the porticoes, a number of pillars that hold up the floor of the loggia above, that is of the second storey." The rooms (partly constructed or altered in the nineteenth century) are thus set on two floors, behind the portico and the upper loggia, save on the short side on the right where there is only the end wall, which in the plan was meant to divide the central peristyle from a rear court with a colonnaded exedra. The design in the *Quattro Libri* also shows that the central block, reserved for the owner and his family, was meant to repeat the colonnade scheme of the courtyard, preceded at the sides by two wings of outbuildings set at right angles to it, with porticoes screened by simple arches borne on pillars and dovecotes.
The date of this building was long uncertain. Some scholars used to relate it to Palladio's early work, in the later 1540s, while others set it among the mature work, at about 1570. Documents that have recently emerged seem to confirm the latter theory and set the start of construction at 1565. But let's take events in their proper order, starting with the client. Marcantonio Sarego, a busy estate-owner, was one of a closely-knit group linked by family ties that at various times commissioned Palladio to design buildings in Verona and the surrounding region (see the entries for the various buildings all called the "Villa Sarego"). The lands at Santa Sofia were given to the family in the late fourteenth century by the overlords of Verona, the Della Scala dynasty. These estates already possessed a large palace with its own chapel, outhouses, etc. Brunoro, the father of Marcantonio, had started to modernize it and in his will of 1536 he required his children to complete the work. But it was only in 1552 that Marcantonio effectively took possession of it, after years of dispute with his brother Annibale over the division of his father's estate. So Palladio's design must be later than this date. In 1555 one of the "marvellous fountains" praised by Palladio was carved and the date set on it, while another had been made about ten years earlier. It was only in 1565 that there is any record of work beginning on a large scale. In May of that year payments were made for the transport of stones "for the building of S. Sofia," scaffolding and other construction materials; but most of the work must have been carried out in 1569, when no fewer than eleven cartloads of stone were brought from the quarry belonging to the family.
It is likely that the new villa was erected on the site of the old manor house and actually incorporated its fourteenth century chapel as well as some of its walls (as appears from studies carried out by using thermoluminescence). The work went beyond the part that has come down to us; a start was made on the right-hand side of the courtyard. In 1740 Francesco Muttoni noted that the form of the whole peristyle had been roughed out and there were two rows of free-standing columns to the east and west, aligned with those now on the site, while on the south side there were only the bases. These features

Drawing with the plan and elevation of the Villa Sarego at Santa Sofia (from the "Quattro Libri").

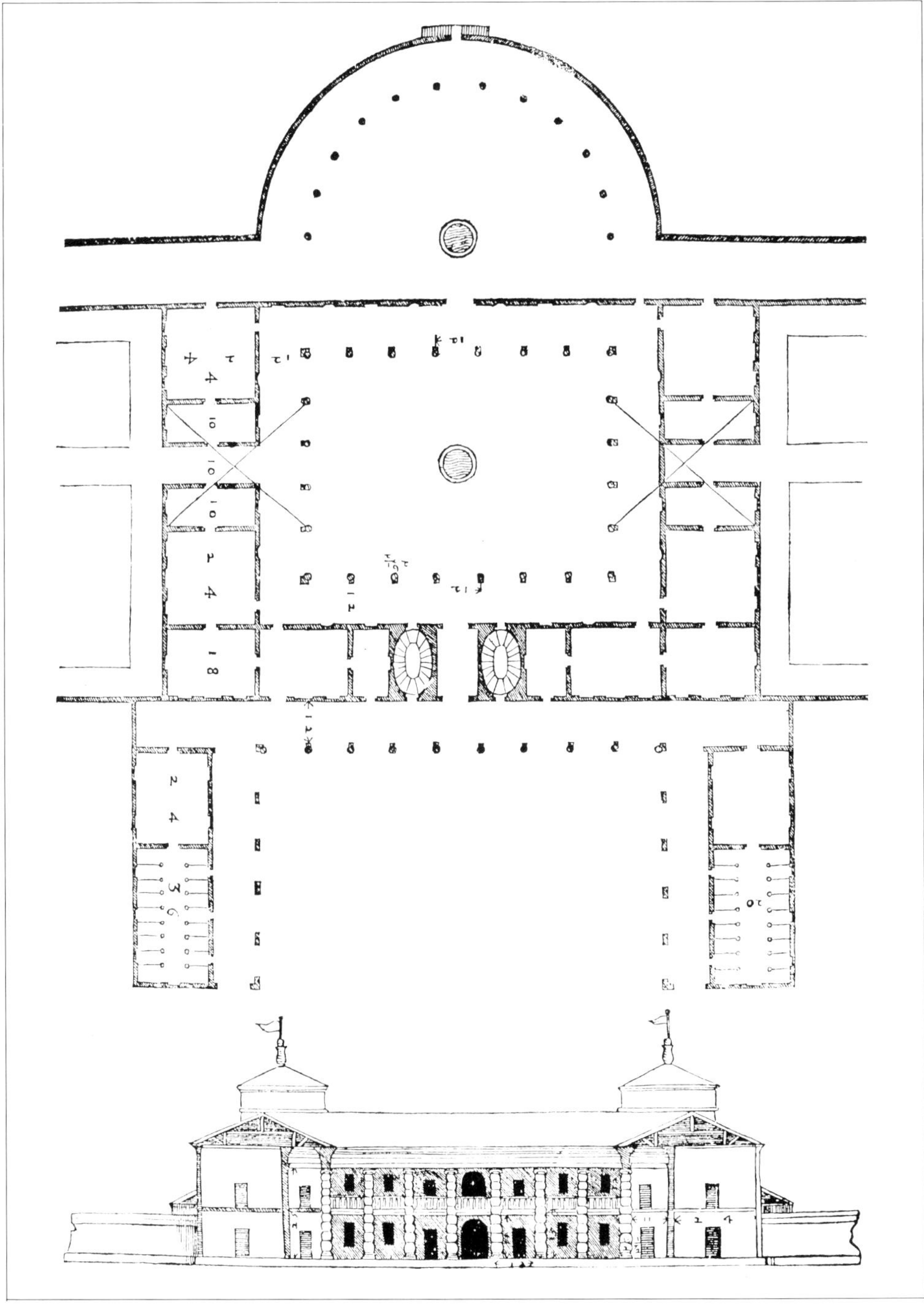

Villa Sarego (Santa Sofia), view of the fragment remaining.

still existed in the mid-nineteenth century, when the fragments were given the present rather disturbing appearance of a completed structure by finishing the vaulting of the portico.

The plan of the Villa Sarego has evident affinities with that of the Villa Thiene at Quinto Vicentino, since both are related to the ideal reconstruction of the Ancient House; but the present work belongs to a later and more mature stage of reflection on the heritage of Roman archaeology, which includes the design for the Villa Mocenigo on the Brenta. Both embody ideas taken from Palladio's study of Roman baths which influenced the design of the Villa Repeta at Campiglia, a building which shows the closest analogies with the composition of the present villa. As for the special use of rustication, the influence here seems not so much that of Giulio Romano as Michele Sanmicheli, particularly his work at Porta Palio at Verona, well advanced by the late 1550s. Some scholars have even suggested that Palladio somehow knew of Bartolomeo Ammannati's work on the layout of the courtyard of the Pitti Palace in Florence from 1561 on.

Bibliography: Palladio, 1570, 1. II, pp. 66-67; Muttoni, 1740, p. 19; Bertotti Scamozzi, 1781, pp. 41-42; Magrini, 1845, p. 240; Biadego, 1886, pp. 15-18; Burger, 1909, pp. 76-83; Gazzola, 1960, pp. 36-37; Pane, 1961, pp. 230-231; Forssman, 1965, pp. 193-194; Ackerman, 1967, pp. 66-68; Zorzi, 1969, pp. 114-119; Cevese, 1973, pp. 57-62; Puppi, 1973, pp. 390-393; Fairbairn, in Burns, 1975, pp. 201-202; Viviani, 1975, pp. 424-428; Borelli, 1976-1977; Marini, in AA.VV., 1980 (IV), pp. 247-256; Rigon, 1980, no. 26; Canova, 1985, pp. 242-250; Muraro, 1986, pp. 296-300; Costant, 1987, pp. 82-84.

Villa Almerico Capra, known as "La Rotonda"

124 Vicenza,
1566; attribution certain.

The villa stands at the start of the Riviera Berica, the road leading southwards out of Vicenza towards Noventa Vicentina. From the road one gets a good view of the right of the building in all its beauty, but the road leading up to it (Via della Rotonda) is about a hundred metres further back. It can be visited from 15 March to 15 October; the exterior can be viewed on Tuesday, Wednesday, and Thursday from 10 a.m. to 12 a.m. and 3 p.m. to 6 p.m.; the interior on Wednesdays at the same hours. For visits by groups of more than ten people at other times, book by telephone (tel. 0444/221793).

This work has been called the epitome of Palladio's architecture: "Form formed by the landscape and forming the landscape." For four centuries it has aroused the admirations of scholars and laymen, and imitations can be found all over the world, Goethe wrote of it: "Perhaps architecture has never attained such a pitch of splendour." The name it has always been known by, "La Rotonda," embodies its essence: it is conceived to be viewed from all sides and even so that one can look out from inside it to allow the gaze to take in a panorama of 360 degrees. "The site is one of the most pleasant and delightful one could find," Palladio wrote in his presentation of the engraving in the *Quattro Libri*, "for it is on a hill easily climbed and washed on one side by the Bacchiglione, a navigable river, and surrounded by other agreeable hills that create the impression of a great amphitheatre, all of which are cultivated and abound in excellent fruits and fine vineyards. So that it may enjoy beautiful views on all sides ... loggias have been set on all four of its façades."
As one walks round the villa, one is surprised to find the Ionic hexastyle pronaos repeated. With its tall flights of steps it opens out towards the countryside, which here slopes gently down to the river (alas, no longer navigable!) and the plain, and there spreads out into a thick wood and the small Valle del Silenzio. Four times the villa repeats its invitation to enter; and once you are inside the domed circular chamber, the heart of the villa, the attraction is reversed, and you are tempted back outside through any one of the four corridors that, like the arms of a Greek cross, divide the cube-shaped prism of the masonry box into four segments, with crystalline geometrical precision, and lead you out to the loggias, the steps and the countryside. And even if you step aside from one of the corridors into the rooms at the side or the corners you still feel drawn to the landscape which lies before you, framed in a window.
So it is the site that generates the forms of the architecture, but this is not all. This is not a "villa-farmhouse," it has no utilitarian purpose; nor is it simply a "villa-belvedere." It was conceived as a true temple to the *otium* of the humanists, the expression of its owner's cultural interests and his ambitions. It revives the archaeological models of pagan shrines of antiquity, like that of Hercules Victor at Tivoli, from which Palladio took not only the centralized form, but even the actual symbols of sacred architecture, the pronaos and (for the first time) the dome, so exalting in this secular building the status of its owners. The Renaissance ideal of man as the measure of all things and the hub of the universe is embodied at the centre of the round domed chamber; it is no accident that the centrally-planned building was regarded as perfect by the architects of that astonishing age. And the orientation of the Rotonda is not, of course, fortuitous: the four corners correspond perfectly to the four cardinal points. This may also have been to allow each of the façades to receive at least a little sunlight, but the origin of this design should be sought in the symbolism of the cosmos, which meant so much to the cultivated society of the age.
So who was the owner of the villa? Palladio dwells at some length on the figure of Paolo Almerico, "A man of the church who was Referendary of two Supreme Pontiffs, Popes Pius IV and V, and who for his merit deserved to be made a Roman Citizen with all his family." And he adds that "this gentleman, after travelling many years from a desire for honour, when all his family were dead returned to his own land." The Canon from Vicenza had indeed had a chequered and adventurous life. Between 1546 and 1548 he was imprisoned in Venice on a charge of murder, later dis-

Drawing with the plan and elevation of the Rotonda (from the "Quattro Libri").

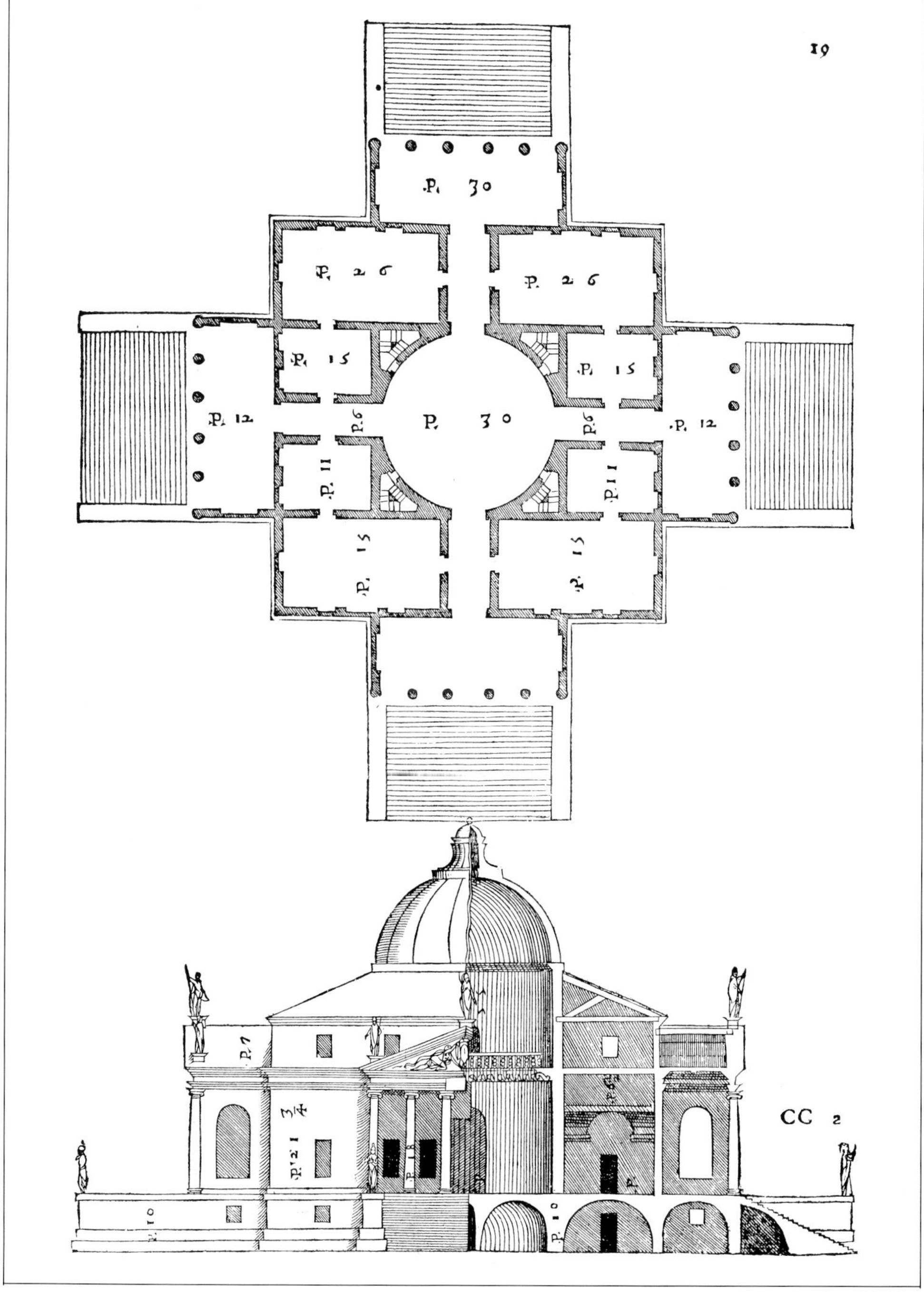

Villa Almerico Capra, La Rotonda, general view and the central circular chamber with frescoes by Ludovico Dorigny.

proved, and after a long controversy with the canons of the cathedral of Vicenza over prebendal questions, he was transferred to the papal court at Rome, though he occasionally returned to his native town. He had long owned land at Ponzano, just outside Vicenza, where the Rotonda was built. Here—perhaps in one of the modest houses he owned, refurbished for the occasion, or perhaps out of doors —he held a reception in 1553 in honour of Isabella Gonzaga, with fireworks as an added attraction. It is pleasant to think that on this occasion he first felt a desire to dwell here in a new, more fitting home. He then slowly began to enlarge the estate by purchasing the adjoining lands. But his work kept him at Rome for more than another decade. Meanwhile he lost his father, his brother and in 1565 his mother, after which—as Palladio tells us—he desired to return home.

The project seems to have taken shape in 1566. After purchasing more land, in October he sold the family palace at Pozzo Rosso in Vicenza for 2,600 ducats, evidently to invest in the new building. La Rotonda was thus not conceived as a second home to be used occasionally but as a substitute for an urban palace. It is no accident that Palladio placed it in the chapter dealing with palaces in the *Quattro Libri*, and this was not just because of its closeness to the city. Construction seems to have started in 1567 and went ahead rapidly—as the poet Magagna tells us in a *Rima* —so that by June 1569 it was definitely occupied by Almerico, who was already calling it "La Rotonda." The next year the statues were also set at the ends of the parapets of the flights of steps, as appears from the fact that the architect refers to them in the *Quattro Libri* as the work of the sculptor Lorenzo Rubini of Vicenza (the one on the right-hand spur of the south-west façade was re-carved after 1848).

No autograph preparatory sketches for the villa have survived, apart from the engraving published in 1570. The completed building varies in some ways from the design. The windows on the *piano nobile* have been enriched with a classical cornice and a small pediment over the window; the width of the main doorways has been reduced; above all the dome is not fully rounded in the building but slightly flattened and covered with a "stepped" roof. There has been much debate over who designed the dome; some scholars attribute it to Vincenzo Scamozzi, who (he himself declared) had a hand in the design after Palladio's death. But it seems that it is definitely by Palladio, who may have considered a fully rounded dome too assertive and violent in relation to the setting, while also exaggerating the height of the circular chamber below. It is also difficult to believe the villa was regarded as inhabitable and the decoration of the interiors begun when the most important chamber still lacked a roof over it. Scamozzi may well have been responsible for the "stepped" arrangement of the tiles, which is found in some of his other works, and also provided openings in the centre of the steps to provide access to the ground floor (rightly closed up again in the eighteenth century by Ottavio Bertotti Scamozzi). At first the dome was open at the top and the rain was collected, in a kind of impluvium, by an opening set in the centre of the paved floor, adorned by the head of faun. The allegorical significance of this has been the subject of many conjectures.

The decoration of the interiors takes the form of stucco work and frescoes. It all forms a single coherent design, so that Palladio was probably involved in its conception. Various different artists worked on it, including some of the outstanding figures of the period, and it can be divided into three phases. From the early 1560s to the death of Almerico in 1589 the sculptural decoration of the corner rooms was completed. It is in all likelihood the work of Ottavio Ridolfi, an artist close to Alessandro Vittoria. Vittoria seems to have been responsible for the stuccoes in the north room, which like those in the dome, differ from the others by the exuberant carving of the tablets, *putti*, curls, sharp projections, masks, etc. Records also seem to show that Vittoria was responsible for the four splendid mantelpieces in the corner rooms (mainly executed by Ridolfi), in different kinds of marble and with the tassels modelled in snowy white stucco to a constant pattern. They were all executed before 1591.

Work presumably started from the east room, where the ceiling is divided up by a broad fascia into segments depicting a triumphal procession, classical in inspiration, in

Villa Almerico Capra, La Rotonda, dome with the frescoes by Alessandro Maganza and stuccoes by Lorenzo Rubini (and sons).

bas-relief against a yellow ground. Refined grotesques painted on a black ground follow the stucco fascia, at the centre of which are frescoes of four female allegorical figures set round a depiction of Virtue triumphing over Vice, attributed to Anselmo Canera. The north room, to the left of the present entrance, is devoted to the celebration of the Arts and is attributed, though very doubtfully, to Bernardino India. Among exuberant stuccoes, in the centre of the ceiling there is a white figure and a serpent biting its tail, a symbol of eternity, together with the three Graces, while around them are set three *tondi* of the Arts and two rectangles with Minerva and Vulcan. Over the door is a panel with what is said to be the portrait of Palladio with the Rotonda as a backdrop. This first phase of the decoration seems to include the grotesques in the four antechambers, attributed to Eliodoro Forbicini, which some scholars suspect were heavily repainted in the eigh-

teenth century. The frescoes in the dome, by Alessandro Maganza, the son of the painter and poet Giambattista Maganza, known as Magagnò, are also probably earlier than those in the remaining two corner rooms. The hollow of the dome is divided by stucco work into eight segments (the execution is attributed to Lorenzo Rubini and his sons Agostino and Virgilio). The four narrower segments, over the corridors, contain niches with stucco figures while above them there is a monochrome painting. The larger segments are each divided into two overlapping panels, splendidly framed, containing allegorical figures whose symbolism is obscure. Other sculptured figures project from the cornice at the base of the dome.

After the death of Paolo Almerico his natural son Virginio at once sold the villa in 1591 to the brothers Odorico and Mario Capra, who set their name on the trabeation of the present pronaos and proceeded to embellish the building. The various stages of work are known thanks to a valuable account book. They completed the parts still unfinished, such as the steps, flooring, plasterwork, the main doorway facing the Riviera Berica, outer walls, cellars and an orangery. Alessandro Maganza was entrusted with the frescoes in the corner rooms to the west and south (1599-1600), which had already been stuccoed. The former is unfortunately in a poor state; it is known as the "Chamber of Religion" and contains at the centre of the ceiling an imposing array of pagan divinities, with below Aristotle, Virgil and the Sybil, coupled with scenes of sacrifices and divination. The second contains Wisdom in the guise of Minerva who overcomes Destiny and Sin and so wins Fame and Fortune. They are accompanied by the representation of various Virtues. The figures in the other panels are refined and of a higher standard. In the same period Giambattista Albanese of Vicenza was commissioned to carve the twelve statues set on the pediments and the crest of the Capra family. The same sculptor, together with his brother Girolamo, carved the fountain with nymphs, the Capra Amalthea, Jove and his eagle, in 1629. The little that remains of it is in the cellars. Between 1645 and 1663 Albanese built the family chapel, on the other side of the road, opposite the entrance. The renovation of the long outhouse that backs onto the present drive leading up to the villa was carried out discreetly, probably by Vincenzo Scamozzi in 1620. The statues crowning it, as well as those in the garden, are attributed to Orazio Marinali.

The final phase covers the late seventeenth and early eighteenth centuries, when the decoration of the central chamber and the four corridors was completed, as well as the various panels over the doors: these are over-elaborate stuccoes by Lombard artists from the Valsolda, and frescoes by Ludovico Dorigny. Dorigny depicted eight enormous Olympian divinities on the walls; their gestures are exaggerated and their drapery over-emphatic, so that together with the illusionistic architectural elements framing them they violate the Palladian spaces in an attempt to involve the viewer that is typically baroque.

Bibliography: Palladio 1570, 1.II, p. 18; Muttoni, 1740, pp. 12 ff.; Bertotti Scamozzi, 1778, pp. 9-13; Magrini, 1845, pp. 78, 238 ff.; Burger, 1909, pp. 53-56; Pane, 1961, pp. 188 ff.; Wittkower, 1964, p. 75; Forssman, 1965, pp. 50-57; Ackerman, 1967, pp. 68-72; Isermayer, 1967; Semenzato, 1968; De Fusco-Scalvini, 1969; Zorzi, 1969, pp. 127-142; Cevese, 1971, I, pp. 153-155 and 1973, pp. 82-85; Puppi, 1973, pp. 380-383; Corboz, 1973, pp. 257-264; Streitz, 1973; Fairbairn, in Burns, 1975, pp. 198-200; Battilotti, 1977, p. 234; Forster, 1980; Rigon, 1980, nos. 24-25; Muraro, 1981-1982; Saccardo, 1982-1987; Canova, 1985, pp. 224-239; Muraro, 1986, pp. 282-295; Bödefeld-Hinz, 1987, pp. 134-138; Costant, 1987, pp. 119-120; AA.VV., 1988.

Villa Sarego

130 Beccacivetta di Coriano, in the commune of Albaredo d'Adige (Verona), 1569; design (?) never built.

See the entry for the Villa Sarego at Miega for instructions how to reach Miega. Then continue on to Michellòrie, in the direction of Albaredo, and then Coriano, on the left. Continue towards the Adige along Via Beccacivetta. There is a fine tree-lined drive leading up the present villa.

On 22 September 1569 Antonio Sarego wrote from Cucca to his brother Federico in Venice, expressing his intention of profiting by Palladio's presence at Miega (a few kilometres away), were he was staying with Antonio's cousin, Annibale Sarego, to invite him to examine a building of theirs at Beccacivetta. This may suggest that the Sarego brothers were thinking of improving the building at Beccacivetta, where they owned large estates; and some scholars see references to this project in a series of letters between them. Actually it is far more likely that they refer to a second bout of work carried out by Palladio at Cucca (see the entry for the Villa Sarego at Cucca). We know he was there on October 4 and received a payment for "making a drawing of the palace," which must mean the old manor house where he had been working since 1564 on the new layout of the courtyard and outhouses. It is quite possible work was also carried out at Beccacivetta, but there is no record of it and no trace of such work in the buildings that still exist there. The present complex is the result of later work; but one of the outhouses in what is known as the "Corte Ricca" (one of two courts around which the complex is organized) contains Cinquecento frescoes with scenes of life in a country house attributed to Domenico Brusasorci, a painter of Verona who also worked on Palladian buildings. This makes it highly likely that Palladio was requested to redesign this building.

Bibliography: Rinaldi Gruber, 1972-1973; Viviani, 1975, pp. 757-760; Franzoni, in AA.VV., 1980 (IV), pp. 250-251.

Villa Porto

Molina di Malo (Vicenza),
1572; attribution not certain, begun only.

From Vicenza take the state highway no. 46 for Schio and then turn right at Malo, in the direction of Thiene. Once you have reached Malo a battlemented wall with a Quattrocento portal appears on the left of the road. The columns stand behind the wall at the end of the courtyard.

One passes through the fine Quattrocento portal in a battlemented wall, suggestive of a castle, and the effect is all the more stunning when one is suddenly faced with a row of giant columns, broken off at various heights. They look like the ruins of ancient Rome, the remains of a great pagan temple transported into the countryside of the upper Vicentine. Instead of which they are the beginning of a huge building never completed. The situation is much the same as when, in the middle of the last century, the *abbé* Antonio Magrini first drew the attention of scholars to this embryo of a villa, with the "foundations buried under annual crops of turnips and beans" and "chipped by the hoe of the peasant." Today there are rows of farm cottages at the sides of the courtyard (which may go back to the early seventeenth century) and the ten shafts rise out of weeds and scrap, while there is no trace of the foundations, at least on the surface.
It is unanimously accepted that these columns belong to a villa designed by Palladio but never built. This is also confirmed by the date 1572 carved on one of the bases (a time when no other architect in the Vicentine was capable of conceiving such an imposingly classical building) and the name of the nobleman accompanying it: Iseppo Porto of Vicenza, for whom Palladio designed a beautiful palace in *contrà* Porti in Vicenza in around 1549. This is also borne out by the affinities with the coeval loggia of the Capitaniato in Piazza dei Signori in Vicenza and the perfect correspondence between the ratio of base to diameter of these columns and the columns of the temple of Jove Stator (i.e. of Castor and Pollux) which Palladio saw in Rome between the Capitol and the Palatine, and which also appears in the last volume of the *Quattro Libri* in his reconstruction of the Corinthian order.
The shafts of these columns—of which only one is still intact up to the drip-ring—are over a metre in diameter, and complete with the capital and entablature would be about 13 metres tall. This alone should give some idea of the grandeur of the building they were designed for. We can make no further conjecture about the nature of the building, save that if it had been completed it would have been one of Palladio's boldest creations, comparable to the Villa Sarego at Santa Sofia di Pedemonte or the design for the Villa Mocenigo on the Brenta.
On the death of his patron in 1581 the estate at Molina was divided equally between his two sons Leonida and Adriano, each of whom thus inherited half of the "plan of the palace," which seems to have got no further than the ruins we see now. An interesting clause in the will laid down that if one of the brothers decided to complete the villa, it would become his property, except for the "passage in the middle," which was to remain their common property to allow the courtyard to be connected with the park at the rear. But work was never resumed and a seventeenth century map (published by Kubelik, 1977, pp. 162-163) still shows the ten free-standing columns and a dark line dividing the great court exactly in half.

Bibliography: Magrini, 1845, p. 294; Zorzi, 1969, pp. 229-230; Cevese, 1971, II, pp. 462-463; Puppi, 1973, p. 400; Kubelik, 1977, II, pp. 162-163; Burns, 1979, pp. 16-18; Mantese, 1988 (who disregards the date 1572 on the base of a column and dates the villa to around 1540).

132

ROUTE NO. 1
1 - Villa Porto
2 - Villino Forni
3 - Villa Godi
4 - Villa Piovene
5 - Villa Porto
6 - Villa Caldogno
ROUTE NO. 2
7 - Villa Gazzotti Grimani
8 - Villa Valmarana
9 - Villa Valmarana
10 - Villa Thiene
11 - Villa Contarini
12 - Villa Thiene
13 - Villa Chiericati
ROUTE NO. 3
14 - Villa Almerico
15 - Villa Repeta
16 - Villa Saraceno
17 - Villa Poiana
18 - Villa Pisani
19 - Villa Badoer
20 - Villa Grimani Molin
ROUTE NO. 4
21 - Villa Trissino
22 - Villa Pisani
23 - Villa Sarego
24 - Villa Sarego
25 - Villa Sarego
ROUTE NO. 5
26 - Villa Angarano
27 - Villa Barbaro
28 - Villa Emo
29 - Villa Cornaro
30 - Villa Foscari
31 - Villa Zeno
BELLUNO
Angarano
Astico
Bassano del Grappa
Asolo
Maser
Lugo
Thiene
Schio
Montecchio Precalcino
Fanzolo
TREVISO
Cessalto
Piave
Livenza
Lake Garda
Molina
Vivaro
Caldogno
Lisiera
Vigardolo
Quinto Vicentino
Piombino Dese
Sile
Santa Sofia
VICENZA
Bertesina
Piazzola sul Brenta
Villafranca Padovana
Vancimuglio
Meledo Alto
Mira
VERONA
Bacchiglione
VENICE
Campiglia dei Berici
PADUA
Bagnolo
Agugliaro
Brenta
Veronella
Pojana Maggiore
Miega
Montagnana
Este
Adige
ROVIGO
Fratta Polesine
Po
Margil

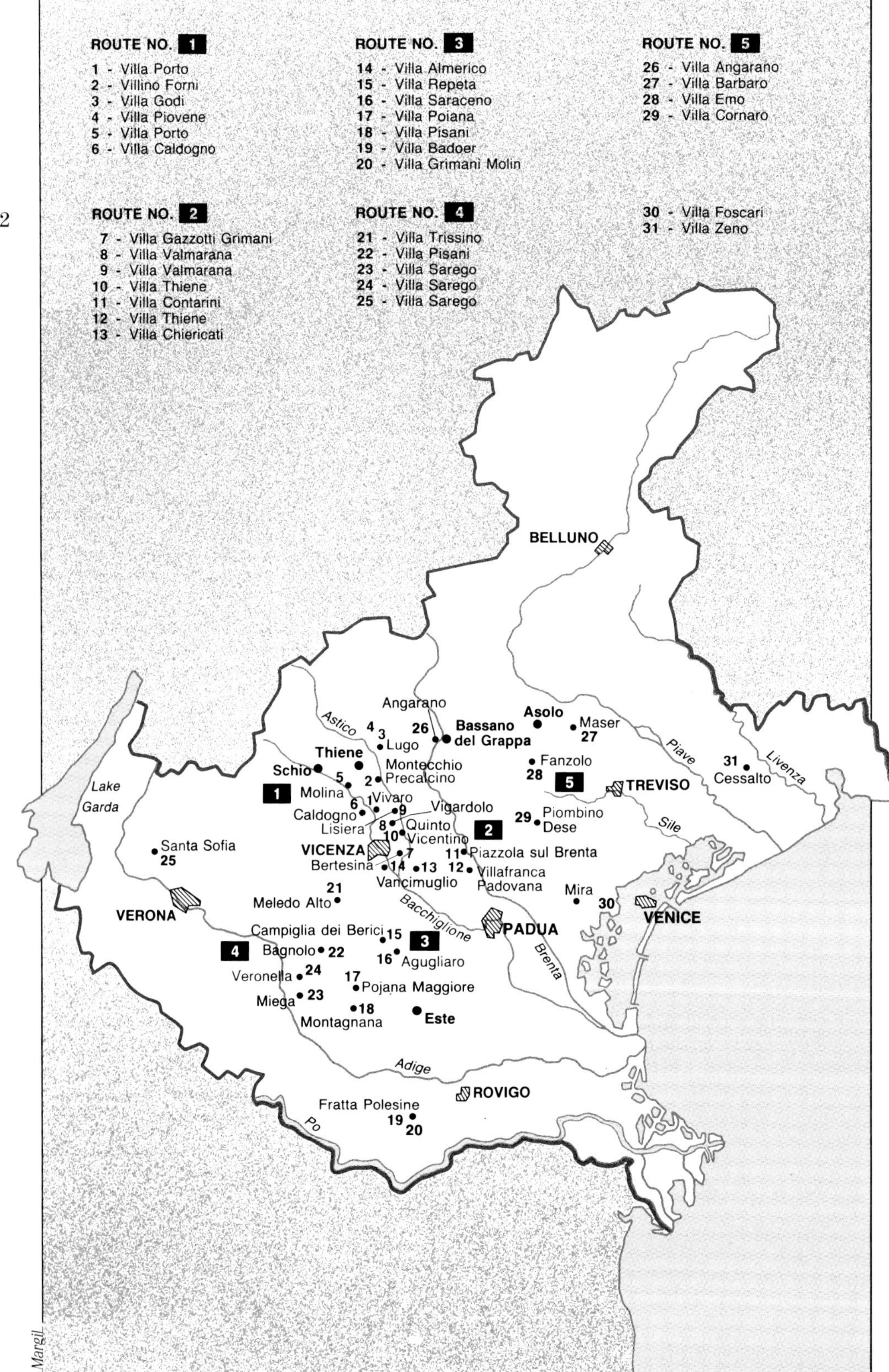

Here I have set out a series of routes taking in groups of villas. Naturally the buildings are not grouped chronologically but by geographical areas. All the tours start from Vicenza and can of course be modified to fit into the time available and suit the traveller's interests. For routes to individual villas and hours of opening, see the fuller entries in this book.

Route 1.
From Vicenza take state highway no. 248 towards Bassano. Just outside the town, on the right, there is the villa of Giangiorgio Trissino at Cricoli (1535-1537). After Polegge turn right along the road for Vivaro, which takes a broad curve and then runs straight all the way to the **Villa Porto.** Return to the highway and go a few kilometres further to Passo di Riva, where you turn left and follow the road which runs along the bank of the river, starting from the bridge over the Astico, and leads to Montecchio Precalcino. At the bend turn left into Via Cerato and after the crossroads, on the right, at no. 7, there is the **Villa Forni.** Return to the crossroads and take the road on the left running north towards Sarcedo. Take the turn-off on the right for the village of Preara where there once stood the **Villa Schio,** of uncertain attribution. From Sarcedo take the road to Zugliano and then to Lugo, where a road climbs up past the **Villa Godi** and ends at the **Villa Piovene.** On the way back to Vicenza it is worth going through Thiene to visit the Quattrocento Porto Colleoni castle, a splendid pre-Palladian villa. On the highway to Vicenza, just outside the built-up area, take the road on the left for Malo. On the way, at Molina, there is a battlemented gateway on the right which leads into a court with columns of the unbuilt **Villa Porto.** Returning to the main road, one finally reaches Caldogno and the **Villa Caldogno** in the centre of the town, near the church.

Route 2.
Start from the small suburb of Bertesina on the north-east of Vicenza. At the side of the church (Via San Cristoforo, 23) there is the early **Villa Gazzotti Grimani.** Then continue to Ospedaletto and highway 53 for Treviso. Turn left almost immediately for Monticello Conte Otto, and keep going until you reach the village of Vigardolo. At the central crossroads turn left for the **Villa Valmarana** in Via Vigardoletto 33. The second **Villa Valmarana,** a mature Palladian work, with its adjoining Quattrocento structures, lies on the highway to Treviso, in the village of Lisiera on the left of the road. Continue a few hundred metres along the highway then turn right straight after crossing the bridge over the Tesina. The road runs parallel with the river before turning sharp left when it reaches the centre of Quinto Vicentino, where the **Villa Thiene** is now the town hall. Continue on towards Gazzo, leaving Lanzé (the site planned for the **Villa Pagliarino**) on your left. Then you come to Piazzola sul Brenta and the enormous baroque **Villa Contarini,** now Villa Simes, with a Cinquecento Palladian building forming its nucleus. From Piazzola continue towards Villafranca Padovana, and about 500 metres before the town, on the right, you will see the rear of the outbuilding of the unfinished **Villa Thiene** at Cicogna. Go through Campodoro and Grisignano di Zocco and so to the state highway which leads back from Padua to Vicenza, on the right of which stands the drive leading to the **Villa Chiericati.**

Route 3.
The first stage of this route is the **Villa Almerico,** famous by its other name of **La Rotonda,** to the south of Vicenza at the start of the Riviera Berica, towards Noventa Vicentina. The road skirts it on the right, but access to the villa is provided by Via della Rotonda a few hundred metres back on the same road. Then return to the main road, leaving on your right Campiglia dei Berici, where the **Villa Repeta** used to stand, on the site of the present seventeenth century building in the centre of the town. On the right there then appears a turn-off for Agugliaro; drive past it and two kilometres further on turn right into Via Finale, flanked by poplars, which runs past the **Villa Saraceno** about 300 metres further on. Drive through Noventa and Pojana Maggiore; just outside the latter, on the road to Montagnana, there is the **Villa Poiana** on the left. At Montagnana you will find the **Villa Pisani** at the point where the road skirting the mediaeval town walls crosses the road running from the town gates towards Padua. Then take the road through

Badia Polesine and Lendinara for Fratta Polesine. Here you can admire the **Villa Badoer** on the far side of the Scortico canal, and on its left the **Villa Grimani Molin,** attributed with some uncertainty to Palladio.

Route 4.
Take the state highway no. 11 from Vicenza to Verona as far as Alte Ceccato, then turn left towards Lonigo. At Meledo (a few kilometres before Sarego), on the other side of the canal flanking the road, there are the two outhouses and the dovecote, much debated works, which stand on the site for which Palladio designed the spectacular **Villa Trissino.** On the right a road turns off for Meledo Alto; half-way up the slope it passes in front of a group of houses which once formed the **Villa Arnaldi,** the residential section being open to visitors inside what is now the second courtyard. Then return to the main road and drive through Lonigo, making for Cologna Veneta, which brings you to Bagnolo. Here, on the far side of the river Guà, there is the **Villa Pisani.** The section of route that follows retraces Palladio's many projects for the Sarego family. We begin with the **Villa Sarego** at Miega, which can be reached by taking the road that runs from Cologna Veneta to Legnano and then turn right when one reaches Caselle. The remains of the villa have disappeared, but behind the church there is a courtyard with segments of the porticoed outhouses. Then continue to the next village, Michellorie. On its left there is Coriano and, at Beccacivetta, a complex once belonging to the Sarego family, which may be the site of a project by Palladio, of which no details remain. Turn off to the right and you come to the old **Villa Sarego** at Veronella, formerly known as Cucca, behind the church. In the forecourt, surrounded by a tall battlemented wall, there are two outhouses set at right angles to each other, by Palladio. There are conjectures that Palladio also worked on another project on a site not far from here, but there is no trace of it. Then make for Verona. From there take the state highway to the northwest towards Rovereto-Trento as far as Parona di Valpolicella. Here continue to the locality called Santa Sofia, before you get to Pedemonte, where you can admire the **Villa Sarego,** in the midst of its very fine park.

Route 5.
From Vicenza drive to Bassano del Grappa; here, in the locality named Angarano, on the far side of the Brenta, there are the outhouses of the **Villa Angarano,** now known as Bianchi Michiel, towards Campese. Then continue through the town for Montebelluna; when you reach the foot of the Asolo hills, take the second turn-off which leads up to this beautiful town; immediately after take the turning to the right, towards Cornuda. This brings you to Maser, where, on the left, stands the very beautiful **Villa Barbaro.** From Maser return directly to the highway, make for Cerano San Marco and then continue towards Castelfranco Veneto, turning off before you find get there for Fanzolo, where you the **Villa Emo.** From Castelfranco take the road towards Venice, which leads you to Piombino Dese, where, on the right, just after the main square, you come to the **Villa Cornaro.**

For the **Villa Foscari,** at La Malcontenta in Mira and the **Villa Zeno** at Cessalto it is advisable to make a separate visit (see the instructions in the relative entries), given the distance separating them from the other villas.

Bibliography

1568

G. Vasari, *Le vite* (ediz. G. Milanesi, vol. VII, Florence 1906).

1570

A. Palladio, *I Quattro Libri dell'Architettura*, Venice.

1740

F. Muttoni, *Architettura di Andrea Palladio Vicentino con le osservazioni dell'Architetto N.N.*, vol. I, Venice.

1761

O. Bertotti Scamozzi, *Il Forestiere istruito...*, Vicenza.

1778

O. Bertotti Scamozzi, *Le fabbriche e i disegni di Andrea Palladio*, vol. II, Vicenza.

T. Temanza, *Vite dei più celebri architetti... veneziani*, Venice (ediz. L. Grassi, Milan 1966).

1781

O. Bertotti Scamozzi, *Le fabbriche e i disegni di Andrea Palladio*, vol. III, Vicenza.

1783

O. Bertotti Scamozzi, *Le fabbriche e i disegni di Andrea Palladio*, vol. IV, Vicenza.

1845

A. Magrini, *Memorie intorno alla vita e le opere di Andrea Palladio*, Padua.

G. Biadego, *Nuovi documenti sopra Andrea Palladio che la prima volta si pubblicano* (for the Boccoli-Zuccoli marriage), Verona.

1909

F. Burger, *Die Villen des Andrea Palladio*, Leipzig.

1925

P. Camerini, *Piazzola*, Milan.

1927

G.K. Lukomski, *Andrea Palladio*, Paris.

1943

A.M. Dalla Pozza, *Andrea Palladio*, Vicenza.

1943-1963

A.M. Dalla Pozza, "Palladiana. VIII-IX," in *Odeo Olimpico*, pp. 99-131.

R. Wittkower, *Architectural Principles in the Age of Humanism*, London (1949)

1950

N. Ivanoff, "Mattia Bortoloni e gli affreschi ignoti della Villa Cornaro a Piombino Dese," in *Arte Veneta*, IV, pp. 123 ff.

1955

G. Masson, "Palladian Villas as rural centers," in *The Architectural Review*, pp. 18 ff.

1956

F. Franco, *Piccola urbanistica della "casa di villa" palladiana, in Venezia e l'Europa*, Atti del XVIII Congresso Internazionale di storia dell'Arte, Venice, pp. 595-598.

R. Gallo, "Andrea Palladio a Venezia," in *Rivista di Venezia*, pp. 26 ff.

1960

AA.VV., *Palladio, Veronese e Vittoria a Maser*, Milano.

P. Gazzola, "Palladio a Verona," in *Bollettino del C.I.S.A.*, II, pp. 34-39.

E. Langenskiöl,"La villa 'La Soranza' di Michele Sanmicheli a Treville di Castelfranco Veneto e lo stile veneziano delle ville," in AA.VV., *Michele Sanmicheli*, Verona, pp. 69-73.

1961

S. Bettini, "Palladio urbanista," in *Arte Veneta*, XV, pp. 89-98.

N. Ivanoff, "Il sacro e il profano negli affreschi di Maser," in *Ateneo Veneto*, no. 145, pp. 51 ff.

R. Pane, *Andrea Palladio*, Turin.

1962

L. Crosato, *Gli affreschi nelle ville venete del Cinquecento*, Treviso.

1963

J.S. Ackerman, "Sources of the Renaissance Villa," in Acts of the Twentieth International Congress of the History of Art (1961), Princeton, pp. 6-18.

G. Mazzotti, *Ville venete*, Rome.

1964

F. Cessi, "L'attività di Alessandro Vittoria a Maser," in *Studi trentini di scienze storiche*, pp. 3-18.

M. Guiotto, "Recenti restauri di edifici palladiani," in *Bollettino del C.I.S.A.*, VI, pp. 78-88.

B. Rupprecht, "Ville venete del '400 e del primo '500: forma e sviluppo," in *Bollettino del C.I.S.A.*, VI, pp. 239-250.

1964-965

A.M. Dalla Pozza, "Palladiana X. XI. XII," in *Odeo Olimpico*, pp. 203-238.

1965

E. Forssman, *Palladios Lehrgebäude*, Uppsala.

G.G. Zorzi, *Le opere pubbliche e i palazzi privati di Andrea Palladio*, Venice.

1966

J.S. Ackerman, *Palladio*, Harmondsworth.

E. Forssman, "Palladio e Daniele Barbaro," in *Bollettino del C.I.S.A.*, VIII, pp. 68-81.

M. Muraro, "Civiltà delle ville venete," in *Arte in Europa. Scritti in onore di Edoardo Arslan*, I, Milan, pp. 533-543.

M. Rosci, "Schemi di ville nel VII libro del Serlio e ville palladiane," in *Bollettino del C.I.S.A.*, VIII, pp. 128-133.

B. Rupprecht, "Villa. Zur Geschichte eines Ideals," in AA.VV., *Probleme der Kunstwissenschaft*, II, Berlin, pp. 120 ff.

1967

J.S. Ackerman, "Palladio's Villas," Glükstadt.
F. Barbieri, "Il primo Palladio," in *Bollettino del C.I.S.A.*, IX, pp. 24-36.
E. Forssman, "Palladio e la pittura a fresco," in *Arte Veneta*, XXI, pp. 71-76.
C.A. Isermeyer, "Die Villa Rotonda von Palladio," in *Zeitschrift für Kunstgeschichte*, pp. 207-221.
N. Ivanoff, *Palladio*, Milan.
G.G. Zorzi, *Le chiese e i ponti di Andrea Palladio*, Venice.

1968

U. Basso, *Cronaca di Maser, delle sue chiese e della villa palladiana dei Barbaro*, Montebelluna.
P. Bieganski, "La struttura architettonica di alcune ville di Palladio in rapporto alla loro funzione pratica," in *Bollettino del C.I.S.A.*, X, pp. 15-30.
R. Cevese, "Considerazioni sulla villa Pisani di Bagnolo," in *Bollettino del C.I.S.A.*, X, pp. 31-41.
R. Cevese (II), "Una scala convessa a villa Poiana," in *Bollettino del C.I.S.A.*, X, pp. 313-314.
C. Fiocco, "Camillo Mariani e Palladio," in *Bollettino del C.I.S.A.*, X, pp. 164-169.
L. Magagnato, "I collaboratori veronesi di Andrea Palladio," in *Bollettino del C.I.S.A.*, X, pp. 170-187.
K. Oberhuber, "H. Cock, Battista Pittoni und Paolo Veronese in Villa Maser," in AA.VV., *Munuscula Discipulorum. Festschrift für Hans Kauffmann zum 70. Geburstag*, Berlin, pp. 207 ff.
K. Oberhuber, "Gli affreschi di Paolo Veronese nella villa Barbaro," in *Bollettino del C.I.S.A.*, X, pp. 188-202.
R. Pallucchini, "Giambattista Zelotti e Giovanni Antonio Fasolo," in *Bollettino del C.I.S.A.*, X, pp. 203-228.
M. Rosci, "Forme e funzioni delle ville venete prepalladiane," in *L'Arte*, no. 2, pp. 27-54.
B. Rupprecht, "L'iconologia nella villa veneta," in *Bollettino del C.I.S.A.*, X, pp. 229-240.
C. Semenzato, "La Rotonda di Vicenza," *Corpus Palladianum*, Vicenza.
W. Timofiewitsch, *Die Sakrale Architektur Palladios*, Munich.
S. Wilinski, "La serliana di villa Poiana a Poiana Maggiore," in *Bollettino del C.I.S.A.*, X, pp. 79-84.
W. Wolters, "Andrea Palladio e la decorazione dei suoi edifici," in *Bollettino del C.I.S.A.*, X, pp. 255-267.

1969

P. Bieganski, "I principii della composizione architettonica di ville palladiane come conseguenza della loro struttura," in *Bollettino del C.I.S.A.*, XI, pp. 195-206.
R. Cevese, "Le ville di Andrea Palladio tra il 1550 e il 1560," in *Bollettino del C.I.S.A.*, XI, pp. 163-173.
R. De Fusco-M.L. Scalvini, "Significanti e significati della Rotonda palladiana," in *op. cit.*, 16, Sept., pp. 5-26.
E. Forssman, "'Del sito da eleggersi per le fabbriche di villa.' Interpretazioni di un testo palladiano," in *Bollettino del C.I.S.A.*, XI, pp. 149-162.
L.H. Heydenreich, "La villa: genesi e sviluppi fino al Palladio," in *Bollettino del C.I.S.A.*, XI, pp. 11-22.
P. Hofer, *Palladios Erstling. Die Villa Godi Valmarana in Lonedo bei Vicenza*, Basel-Stuttgart.
W. Prinz, "La 'sala di quattro colonne' nell'opera di Palladio," in *Bollettino del C.I.S.A.*, XI, pp. 370-386.
L. Puppi, "Rassegna degli studi sulle ville venete (1952-1969)," in *L'Arte*, nos. 7-8, pp. 215-226.
F. Rigon, "Torri medievali come primi nuclei di insediamento di villa," in *Bollettino del C.I.S.A.*, XI, pp. 387-392.
M. Rosci, "Ville rustiche del Quattrocento veneto," in *Bollettino del C.I.S.A.*, XI, pp. 78-82.
M. Tafuri, "Committenza e tipologia nelle ville palladiane," in *Bollettino del C.I.S.A.*, XI, pp. 120-136.
A. Ventura, "Aspetti storico-economici della villa veneta," in *Bollettino del C.I.S.A.*, XI, pp. 65-77.
W. Wolters, "Sebastiano Serlio e il suo contributo alla villa veneziana prima del Palladio," in *Bollettino del C.I.S.A.*, XI, pp. 83-94.
M.A. Zancan, "Le ville vicentine del Quattrocento," in *Bollettino del C.I.S.A.*, XI, pp. 430-446.
G.G. Zorzi, *Le ville e i teatri di Andrea Palladio*, Venice.

1970

F. Barbieri, "Palladio in villa negli anni quaranta: da Lonedo a Bagnolo," in *Arte Veneta*, XXIV, pp. 63-79.
R. Bentmann-M. Müller, *Die Villa als Herrschaftsarchitektur*, Frankfurt am Main.
G.P. Bordignon Favero, "La villa Emo di Fanzolo," *Corpus Palladianum*, Vicenza.
N. Ivanoff, "La tematica degli affreschi di Maser," in *Arte Veneta*, XXIV, pp. 210-213.
M. Rosci, "Rassegna degli studi palladiani (1959-1969)," in *L'Arte*, pp. 114-124.

1971

F. Barbieri, "Palladio come stimolo all'architettura neoclassica: lo 'specimen' della villa di Quinto," in *Bollettino del C.I.S.A.*, XIII, pp. 43-54.
A. Canova, *Ville del Polesine*, Rovigo.
R. Cevese, *Ville della provincia di Vicenza*, 2 vols., Milan.
J. Harris, "Three Unrecorded Palladio Designs from Inigo Jones's Collection," in *The Burlington Magazine*, pp. 34-37.
L. Puppi, "Un letterato in villa: Giangiorgio Trissino a Cricoli," in *Arte Veneta*, XXV, pp. 79-91.

1972

R. Bentmann-M. Müller, "Materialien zur Italie-

nischen Villa der Renaissance," in *Architectura*, pp. 169 ff.
P. Bieganski, "Spazi e planimetrie nella villa palladiana," in *Bollettino del C.I.S.A.*, XIV, pp. 151-164.
R. Cocke, "Veronese and Daniele Barbaro: the Decoration of Villa Maser," in *Journal of the Warburg and Courtauld Institutes*, XXXV, pp. 226-246.
D. Lewis, "La datazione della villa Corner a Piombino Dese," in *Bollettino del C.I.S.A.*, XIV, pp. 381-393.
L. Puppi, "La villa Badoer di Fratta Polesine," *Corpus Palladianum*, Vicenza.
L. Puppi (II), "Palladio e l'ambiente naturale e storico," in *Bollettino del C.I.S.A.*, XIV, pp. 225-234.

1972-1973

A. Rinaldi Gruber, "Una interessante scoperta artistica a Beccacivetta di Coriano Veronese," in *Atti e Memorie dell'Accademia di SS.LL.AA. di Verona*, pp. 138-202.

1973

AA.VV., *Mostra del Palladio*, Catalogue, Milan.
F. Barbieri, "Palladio in villa 1973," in *Bollettino del C.I.S.A.*, XV, pp. 193-209.
R. Cevese, "L'opera del Palladio," in AA.VV., *Mostra del Palladio*, Milan.
E. Forssman, *Visible Harmony, Palladio's Villa Foscari at Malcontenta*, Stockholm.
D. Lewis, "Disegni autografi del Palladio: le piante per Caldogno e Maser 1548-1549," in *Bollettino del C.I.S.A.*, XV, pp. 369-379.
W. Prinz, *Anfänge des oberitalienischen Villenbaues*, edited by the Art History Institute, University of Frankfurt.
L. Puppi, *Andrea Palladio*, Milan.
C. Semenzato, *Villa Simes già Contarini*, Milan.
R. Streitz, *Palladio. La Rotonde et sa géométrie*, Lausanne-Paris.
G. Suitner Nicolini, "Per una lettura urbanistica delle ville venete. Proposta di una tipologia territoriale," in *Bollettino del C.I.S.A.*, XV, pp. 447-465.

1974

F. Barbieri, "Il teatro Olimpico: dalla città esistenziale alla città ideale," in *Bollettino del C.I.S.A.*, XVI, pp. 309-322.
P. Fancelli, *Palladio e Preneste*, Rome.
N. Huse, "Palladio und die Villa Barbaro in Maser: Bemerkungen zum Problem der Autorschaft," in *Arte Veneta*, XXVIII, pp. 106-122.
M. Kubelik, "Gli edifici palladiani nei disegni del magistrato veneto dei Beni Inculti," in *Bollettino del C.I.S.A.*, XVI, pp. 445-465.
L. Puppi, "Dubbi e certezze per Palladio costruttore in villa," in *Arte Veneta*, XXVIII, pp. 95-105.

1975

H. Burns, *Andrea Palladio 1508-1580. The portico and the farmyard Catalogue*, London.
D. Lewis, "Girolamo II Corner's completion of Piombino (with an unrecognized building of 1593 by Vincenzo Scamozzi)," in *Bollettino del C.I.S.A.*, XVII, pp. 401-405.
L. Puppi, "Una conferma per Palladio: villa Contarini-Camerini a Piazzola sul Brenta," in *Storia architettura*, no. 3, Sept.-Dec., pp. 13-18.
C. Semenzato, *Le ville del Polesine*, Vicenza.
G.F. Viviani, *La villa nel Veronese*, Verona.

1976

U. Basso, *La villa e il tempietto dei Barbaro a Maser*, Montebelluna.
M. Magnani Cianetti, "Palladio e l'antico: le ville venete e la cultura antiquaria rinascimentale," in *Quaderni dell'Istituto di Storia dell'Architettura*, II, pp. 71-94.
T. Pignatti, *Veronese. L'opera completa*, Venice.
L. Puppi, "Novità per Michele Sanmicheli e Vincenzo Scamozzi, 'appresso' Palladio," in *Storia dell'arte*, no. 26, pp. 12-22.
S. Ray, "Un problema aperto: alle radici di Palladio," in *L'Architettura*, pp. 248 ff.

1976-1977

G. Borelli, "Terra e patrizi nel XVI secolo: Marcantonio Sarego," in *Studi Storici Luigi Simeoni*, pp. 43-73.

1977

D. Battilotti, "Nuovi documenti per Palladio (with an archival appendix on Fasolo)," in *Arte Veneta*, XXXI, pp. 232-239.
U. Berger, "Die Villa Thiene in Quinto. Ein wiedergefundenes Frühwerk Palladios," in *Arte Veneta*, XXXI, pp. 80-94.
M. Kubelik, *Die Villa im Veneto*, Munich.
W. Oechslin, "Die Villa Barbaro in Maser," in *Palladio in der Architektur des Vicentino*, Rome, pp. 62-63.
R. Smith, "A matter of choices: Veronese, Palladio and Barbaro," in *Arte Veneta*, XXXI, pp. 61 ff.
G.B. Tiozzo, *Le ville del Brenta*, Venice.

1978

U. Berger, *Palladios Frühwerk*, Berlin.
G.P. Bordignon Favero, "Una precisazione sul committente di villa Emo a Fanzolo," in *Bollettino del C.I.S.A.*, XX, pp. 225-236.
A. Corboz, "L'articolazione verticale degli spazi nelle ville palladiane," in *Bollettino del C.I.S.A.*, XX, pp. 129-143.
L. Crosato Larcher, "Postille alla lettura del ciclo della Malcontenta dopo il restauro," in *Arte Veneta*, XXXII, pp. 223 ff.
A. Foscari, "Malcontenta, il restauro delle facciate," in *Bollettino del C.I.S.A.*, pp. 273-282.
D. Gioseffi, "Dal progetto al trattato: incontro e scontro con la realtà," in *Bollettino del C.I.S.A.*, XX, pp. 27-45.
C.A. Isermeyer, "Ein Bildnis Palladios und eine frühe Ansicht der Villa Rotonda," in AA.VV., *Fest-*

schrift Herbert Siehenhümer, Würzburg.
M. Muraro, "Feudo e ville venete," in *Bollettino del C.I.S.A.*, XX, pp. 203-223.
A. Pereswet Soltan, "Il restauro della villa Pisani, ora Ferri, a Bagnolo," in *Bollettino del C.I.S.A.*, XX, pp. 283-296.
L. Puppi, "Palladio in cantiere," in *Bollettino del C.I.S.A.*, XX, pp. 157-170.

1979

F. Barbieri, "Trissino e Palladio," in *Bollettino del C.I.S.A.*, XXI, pp. 35-39.
H. Burns, "Le opere minori del Palladio," in *Bollettino del C.I.S.A.*, XXI, pp. 9-34.
H. Burns (II), "Suggerimenti per l'identificazione di alcuni progetti e schizzi palladiani," in *Bollettino del C.I.S.A.*, XXI, pp. 113-140.
D.R. Coffin, *The Villa in the Life of Renaissance Rome*, Princeton.
M. Kubelik, "Per una nuova lettura del secondo libro di Andrea Palladio," in *Bollettino del C.I.S.A.*, XXI, pp. 117-197.
L. Puppi, "Professione e professionalità in Palladio," in *Il Veltro*, pp. 559-574.

1979-1980

D. Battilotti, "Nuovi contributi archivistici per Palladio," in *Atti dell'Istituto Veneto di SS.LL.AA.*, pp. 199-218.

1980

AA.VV., *Alvise Cornaro e il suo tempo*, Exhibition Catalogue, Padua.
AA.VV. (II), *Andrea Palladio. Il testo, l'immagine, la città*, Exhibition Catalogue, Milan.
AA.VV. (III), *Architettura e utopia nella Venezia del '500*, Exhibition Catalogue, Milan.
AA.VV. (IV), *Palladio e Verona*, Exhibition Catalogue, Milan.
AA.VV. (V), *Palladio: la sua eredità nel mondo*, Exhibition Catalogue, Milan.
AA.VV. (VI), *"Testimonianze veneziane di interesse palladiano,"* Exhibition Catalogue, Venice.
F. Barbieri, "Aspetti del Palladio 'urbanista': la scena vicentina," in *Bollettino del C.I.S.A.*, XXII/I, pp. 119-135.
D. Battilotti, *Vicenza al tempo di Andrea Palladio attraverso i libri dell'estimo del 1563-1564*, Vicenza.
P. Bieganski, "Teoria e pratica del Palladio nelle concezioni spaziali delle ville," in *Bollettino del C.I.S.A.*, XXII/I, pp. 297-307.
R. Cevese, "Andrea Palladio architetto nella bottega di Pedemuro," in *Bollettino del C.I.S.A.*, XXII, pp. 159-166.
R. Cevese (II), *Invito a Palladio*, Milan.
K.W. Forster, "Is Palladio's Villa Rotonda an Architectural Novelty?," in AA.VV., *Palladio, ein Symposium*, Einsiedeln, pp. 27-34.
D. Ch. Goedicke-K. Slusallek-M. Kubelik, "Primi risultati sulla datazione di alcune ville palladiane grazie alla termoluminescenza (TL)," in *Bollettino del C.I.S.A.*, XXII/I, pp. 97-118.
M. Guiotto, "Architetture di Andrea Palladio nella Riviera del Brenta," in *Bollettino del C.I.S.A.*, XXII/II, pp. 139- 146.
D. Lewis, "Il significato della decorazione plastica e pittorica a Maser," in *Bollettino del C.I.S.A.*, XXII/I, pp. 203-213.
M. Muraro, *La villa palladiana dei Repeta a Campiglia dei Berici*, Campiglia dei Berici.
A. Palladio, *I Quattro Libri dell'Architettura*, edited by L. Magagnato and P. Marini, Milan.
W. Prinz, "Appunti sulla relazione ideale tra la villa Rotonda e il cosmo, nonché alcune osservazioni su un mascherone posto al centro del pavimento della sala," in *Bollettino del C.I.S.A.*, XXII/I, pp. 279-287.
L. Puppi, "Per Paolo Veronese architetto. Un documento inedito, una firma e uno strano silenzio di Palladio," in *Palladio*, 1/4, pp. 53-76.
L. Puppi, "Venezia: architettura, città e territorio tra la fine del '400 e l'avvio del '500," in AA.VV., *Florence and Venice: comparisons and relations*, Florence, pp. 341-355.
T. Puttfarken, "Bacchus und Hymenaeus: Bemerkungen zu zwei Fresken von Veronese in der Villa Barbaro in Maser," in *Mitteilungen des Kunsthistorischen Institutes in Florenz*, pp. 1-14.
F. Rigon, *Palladio*, Bologna.
U. Soragni, "Economia neo-feudale e dialettica del territorio nelle ville venete," in *Bollettino del C.I.S.A.*, XXII, pp. 137-146.

1981

D. Lewis, *The Drawings of Andrea Palladio*, Washington, D.C.
T.A. Marder, "La dedica e la funzione del tempietto di Palladio a Maser," in *Bollettino del C.I.S.A.*, XXIII, pp. 241- 246.
A. Olivieri, *Palladio, le corti e le famiglie*, Vicenza.
G.B. Tiozzo, *Il Palladio e le ville fluviali*, Venice.

1981-1982

M. Muraro, "Andrea Palladio e la committenza signorile nel Basso Vicentino," in *Odeo Olimpico*, pp. 33-45.

1982

AA.VV., *Palladio e Venezia*, edited by L. Puppi, Florence.
L. Crosato Larcher, "Considerazioni sul programma iconografico di Maser," in *Mitteilungen des Kunsthistorischen Institutes in Florenz*, pp. 211-256.
L. Puppi, *Andrea Palladio*, German edit., Munich.

1982-1987

M. Saccardo, "Il perfezionamento della Rotonda promosso da Odorico e Mario Capra (1591-1619)," in *Bollettino del C.I.S.A.*, XXIV, pp. 161-210.

1983

D. Battilotti-L. Puppi, "Prime approssimazioni su Giambattista Ponchini," in *Ricerche di Storia dell'arte*, pp. 77-83.
A. Foscari-M. Tafuri, *L'armonia e i conflitti. La chiesa di S. Francesco della Vigna nella Venezia del '500*, Turin.
G. Barbieri, *Andrea Palladio e la cultura veneta del Rinascimento*, Rome.

1984

AA.VV., *Palladio e Palladianesimo in Polesine*, Rovigo.
M. Azzi Visentini, *L'Orto Botanico di Padova e il giardino del Rinascimento*, Milan.
C.J. Kolb, "New Evidence for Villa Pisani at Montagnana," in AA.VV., *Interpretazioni veneziane. Studi di storia dell'arte in onore di Michelangelo Muraro*, Venice, pp. 227-237.

1985

D. Battilotti, "Villa Barbaro a Maser: un difficile cantiere," in *Storia dell'Arte*, pp. 33-48.
A. Canova, *Le ville del Palladio*, Treviso.

1986

M. Muraro, *Civiltà delle ville venete*, Udine.

1987

E. Bassi, *Ville della provincia di Venezia*, Milan.
G. Bödefeld-B. Hinz, *Die Villen im Veneto*, Cologne.
T. Carunchio-I. Cavaggioni-C. Del Zoppo, *La villa Saraceno a Finale di Agugliaro*, Vicenza.
C. Costant, *Guide Palladio. Vicence, Venise, la Vénétie*, Paris.
L. Puppi, "Palladio e Leonardo Mocenigo. Un palazzo a Padova, una villa 'per un... sito sopra la Brenta', e una questione di metodo," in AA.VV., *Klassizismus. Epoche und Probleme. Festschrift für Erik Forssman*, Hildesheim-Zürich-New York, pp. 337-362.

1988

AA.VV., "La Rotonda," *Corpus Palladianum*, Milan.
A. Palladio, *Scritti sull'architettura (1554-1579)*, edited by L. Puppi, Vicenza.

1989

G. Mantese, "L'incompiuta villa palladiana Da Porto in Molina di Malo," in *Andrea Palladio. Studi recenti 1959-1988*, Atti del seminario del C.I.S.A., 1988 (soon to be published).
A. Rinaldi, "Tra 'locus' e testo: villa Badoer nei 'Quattro Libri' di Andrea Palladio," in *QUA.S.A.R.* (Quaderni di Storia dell'architettura e Restauro), no. 1, pp. 23-30.
G. Zaupa, *Andrea Palladio e la sua committenza. Architettura e denaro nel '500*, Rome-Reggio Calabria.

Printed for Electa by Fantonigrafica - Elemond Editori Associati